My First Book Of Patterns

Pencil Control

With Coloring and Illustrated Activities

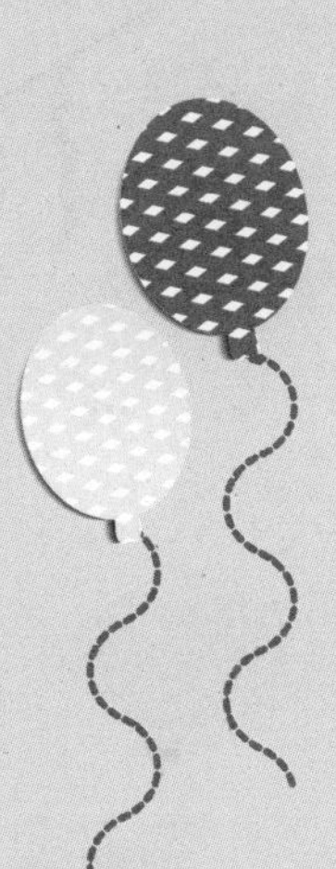

This book belongs to

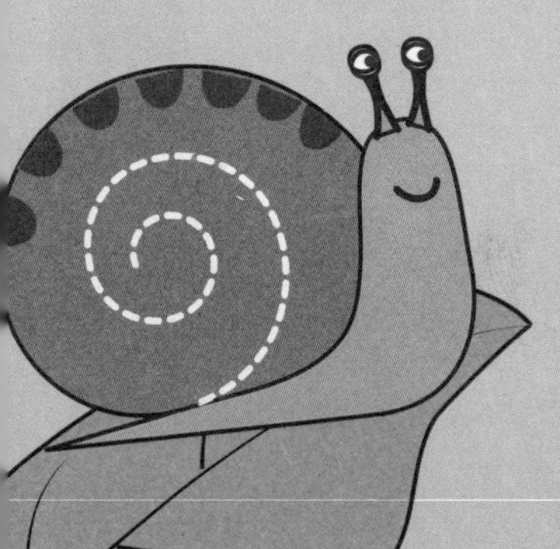

Standing Lines

Trace the dotted lines from top to bottom.

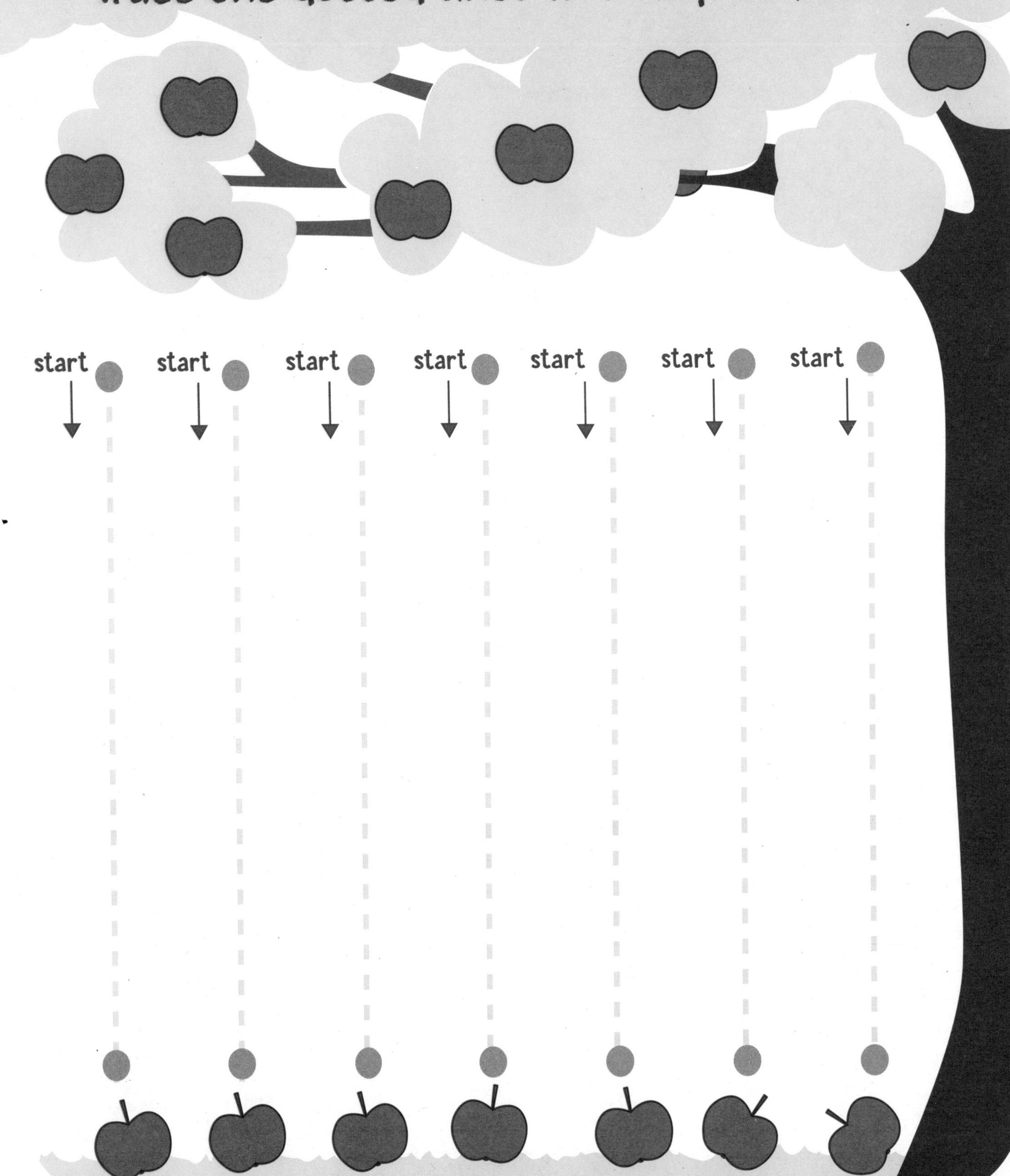

Sleeping Lines

Trace the dotted lines from left to right.

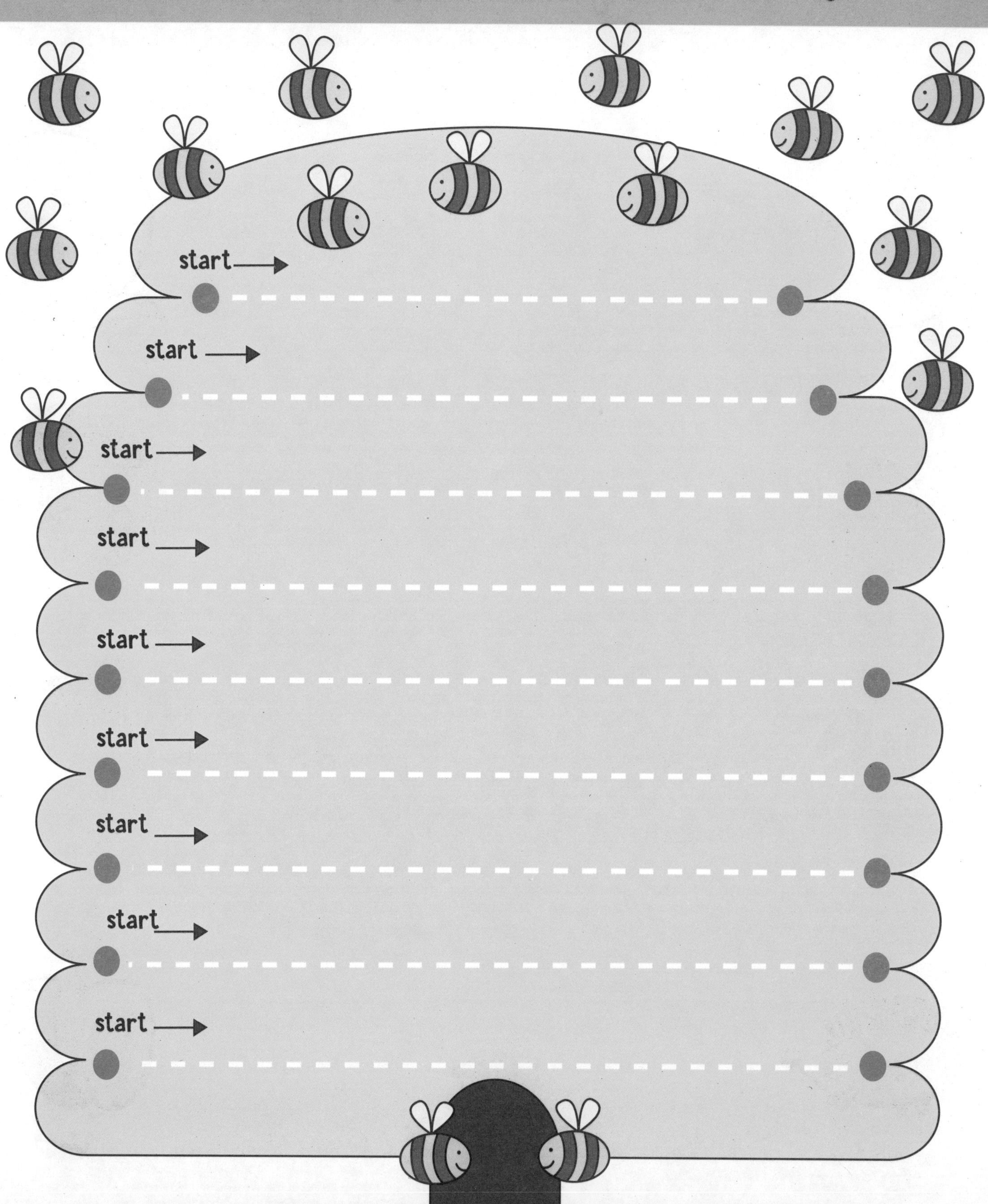

Food Search

Help the animals reach their favorite food by joining the dotted lines.

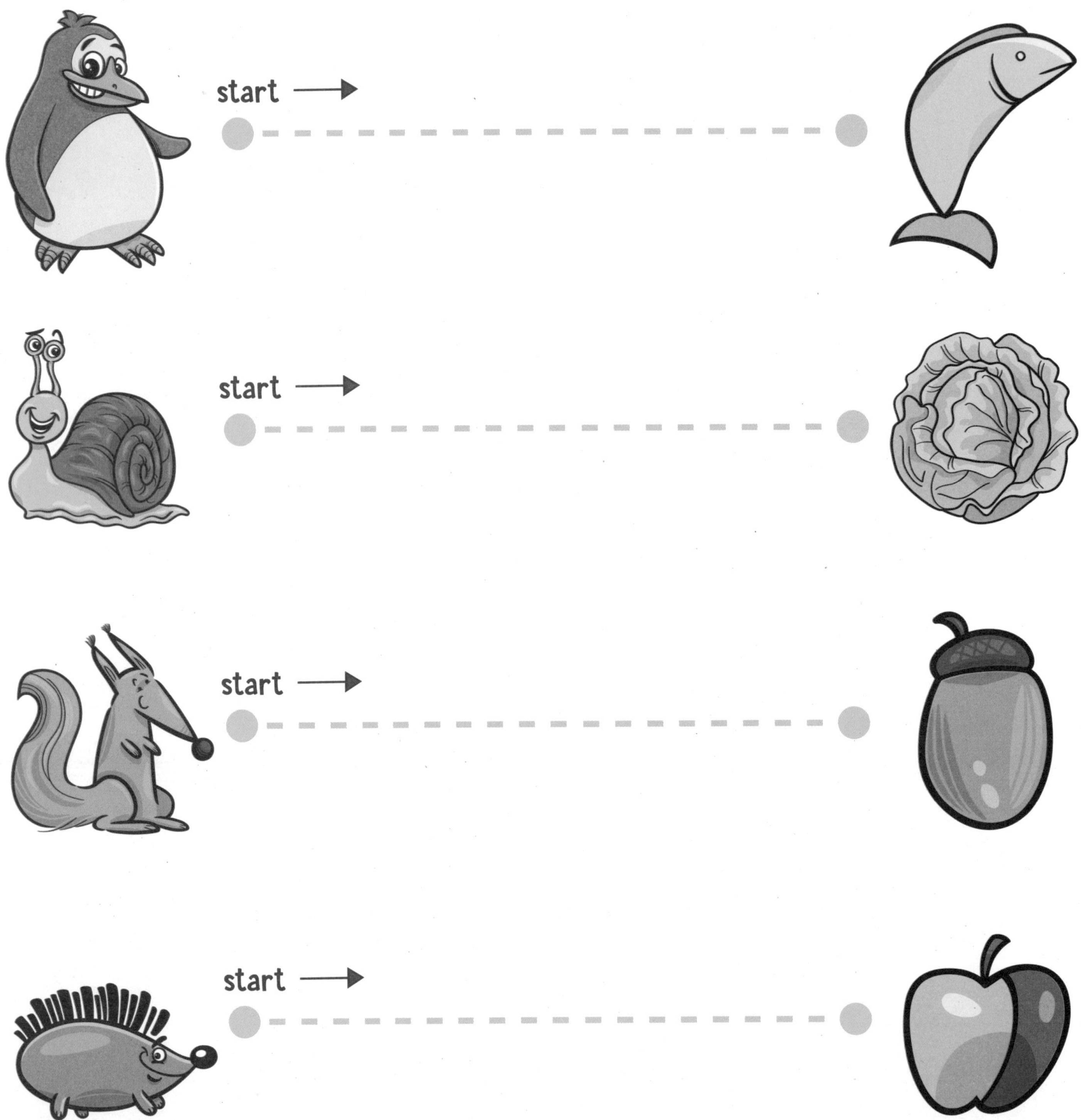

Dog Path

Help the dog reach his home by drawing a line within the path given below.

Slanting Lines

Trace the dotted lines on the branch.

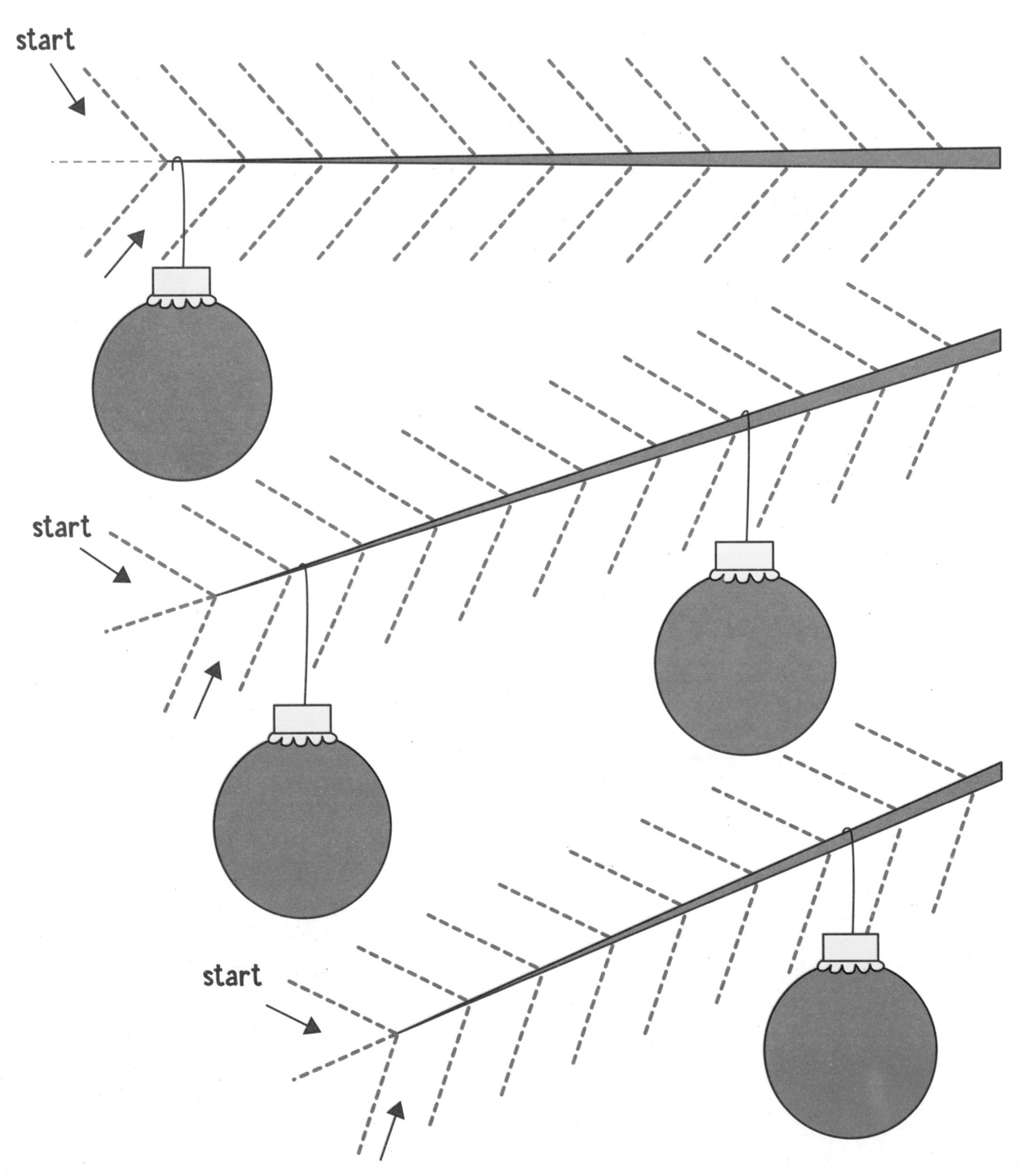

Zig-Zag Lines

Trace the dotted lines on the crocodile's back.

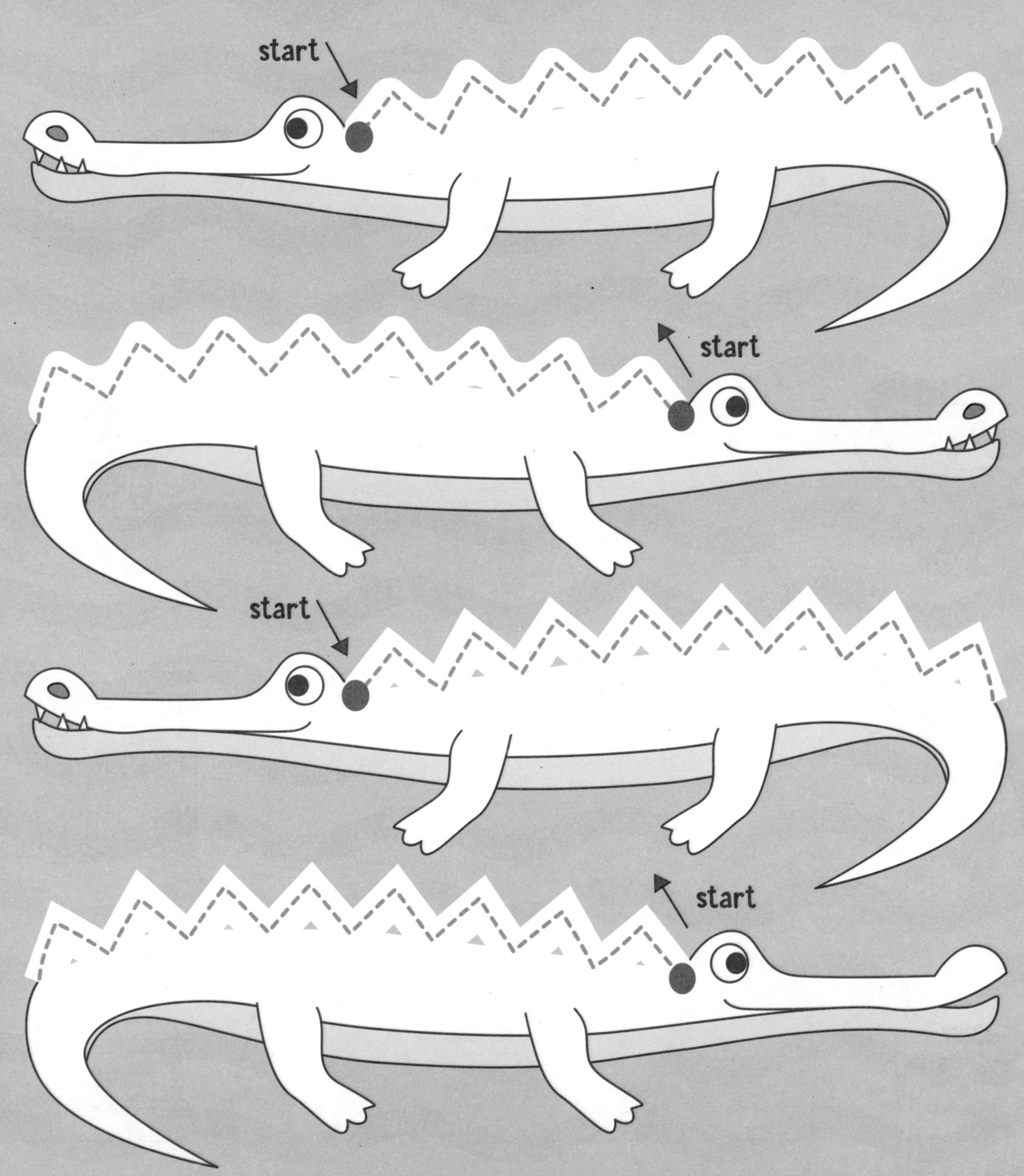

Way to Home

Trace the lines from the animals to their homes.

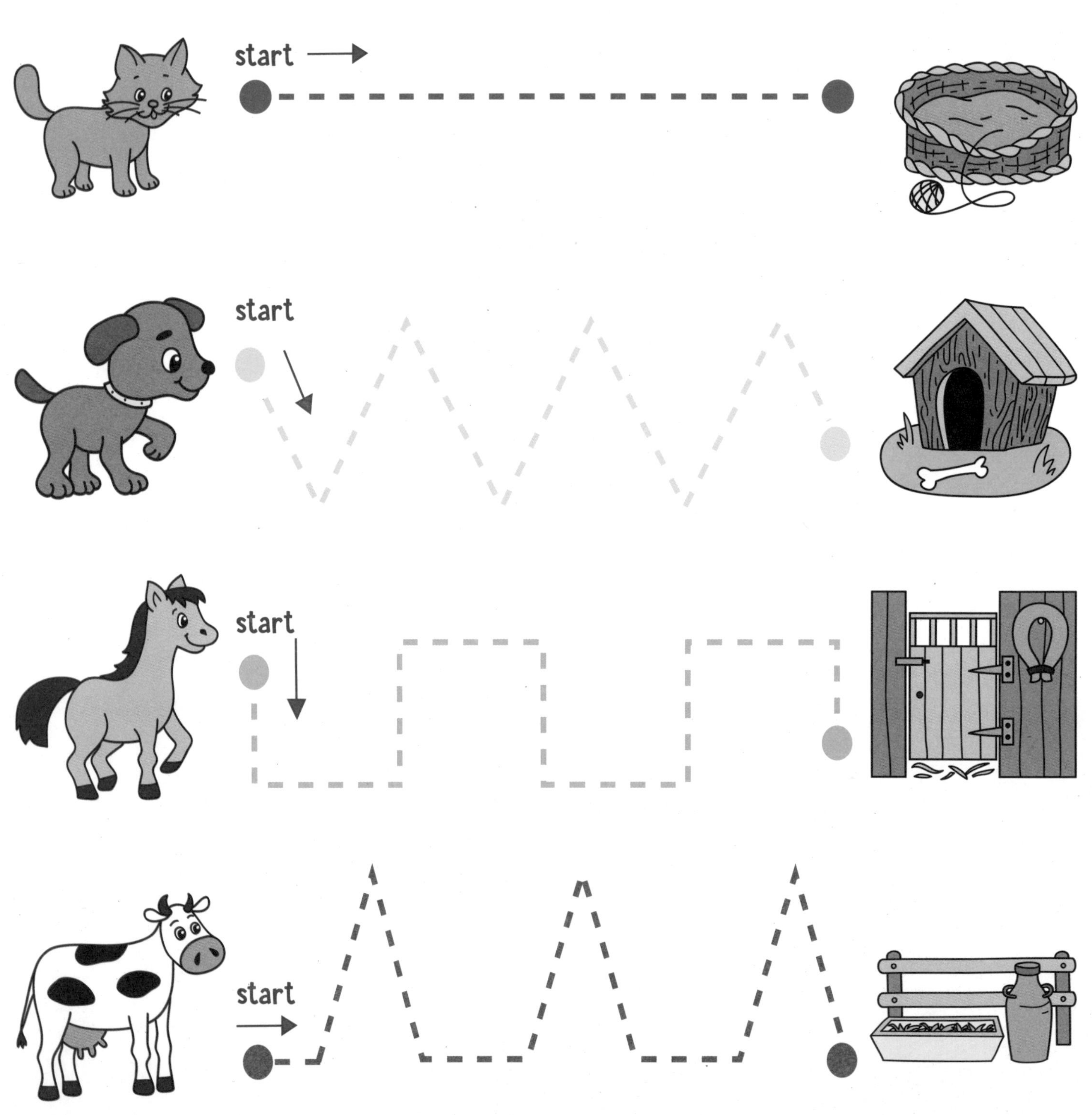

Friends Forever

Trace the dotted lines and help the friends meet.

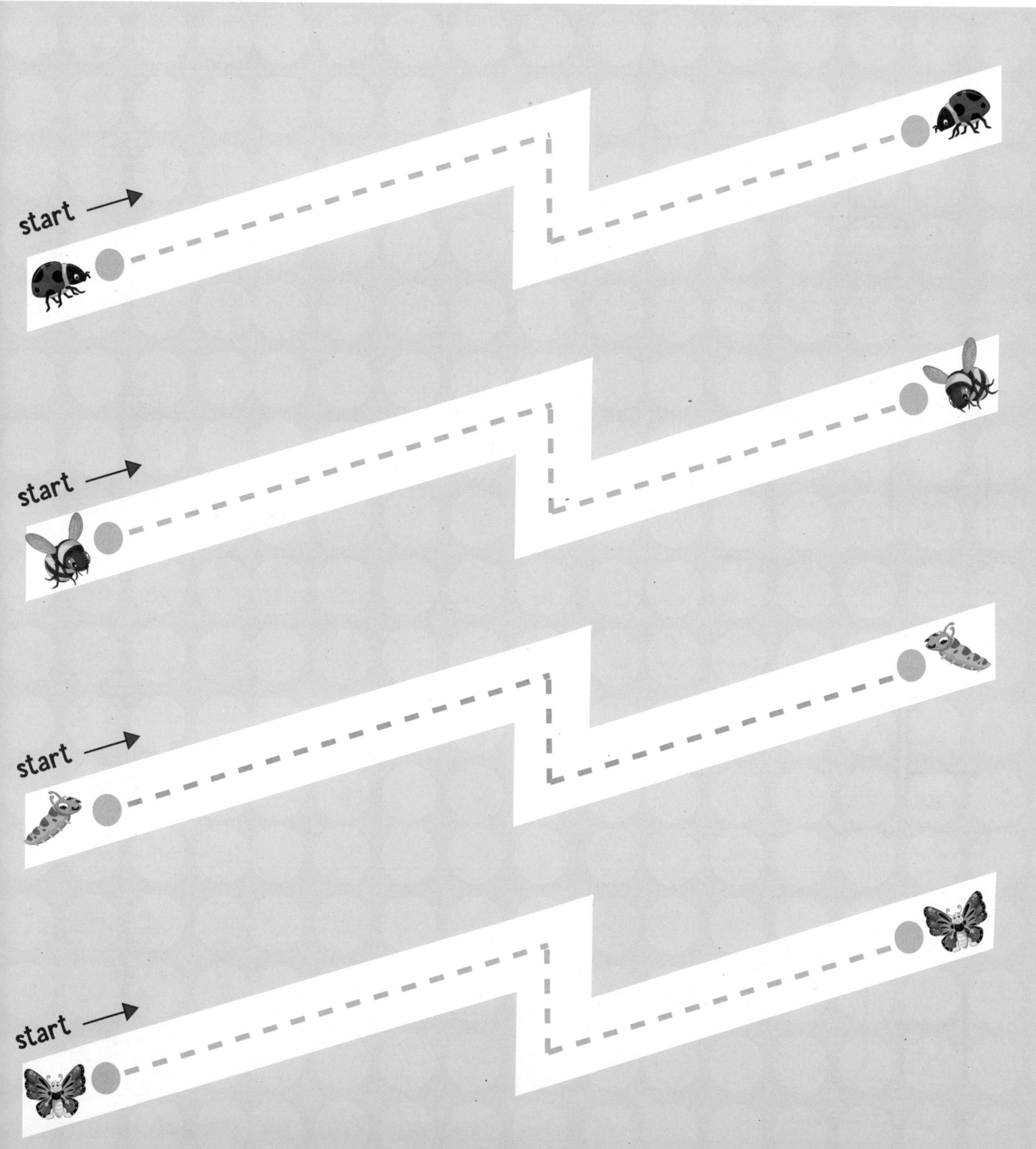

Curved Lines

Trace the lines up and down. Help the ship reach the light house.

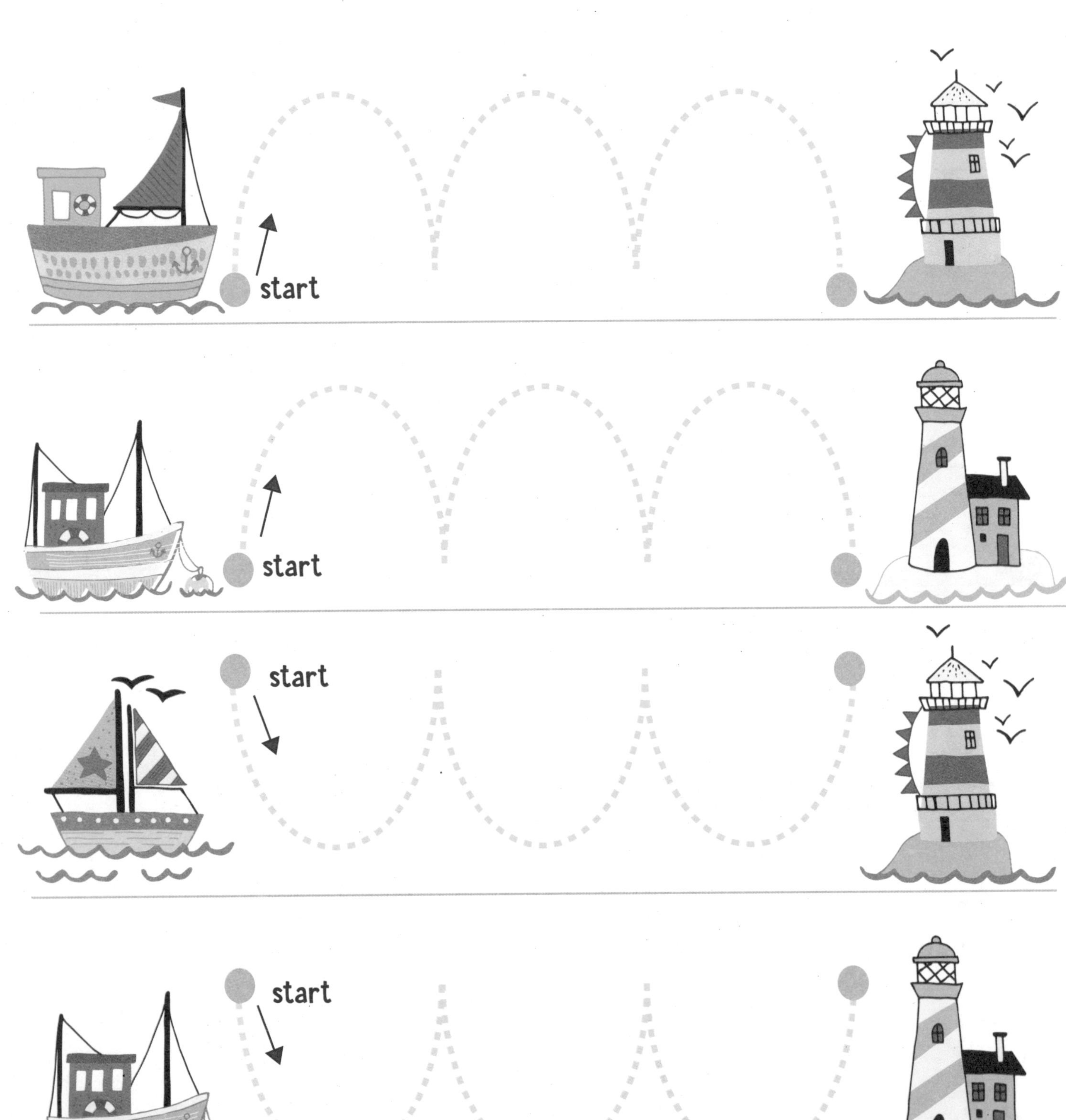

Wavy Lines

Trace the wavy lines to match the pictures.

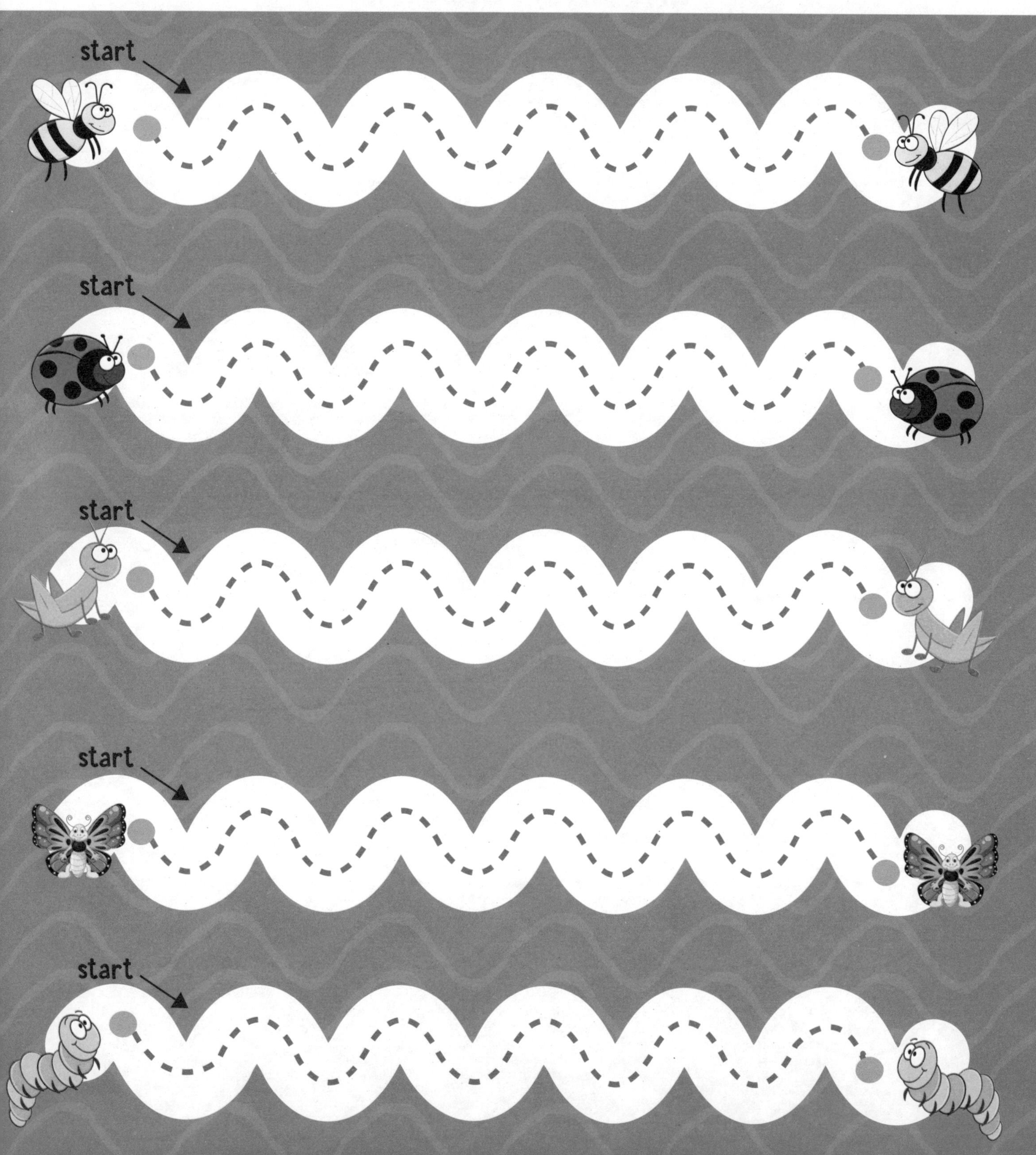

Sailing Ship

Trace the dotted lines to finish the picture and then color it.

Curved Lines

Trace the dotted lines to complete the picture.

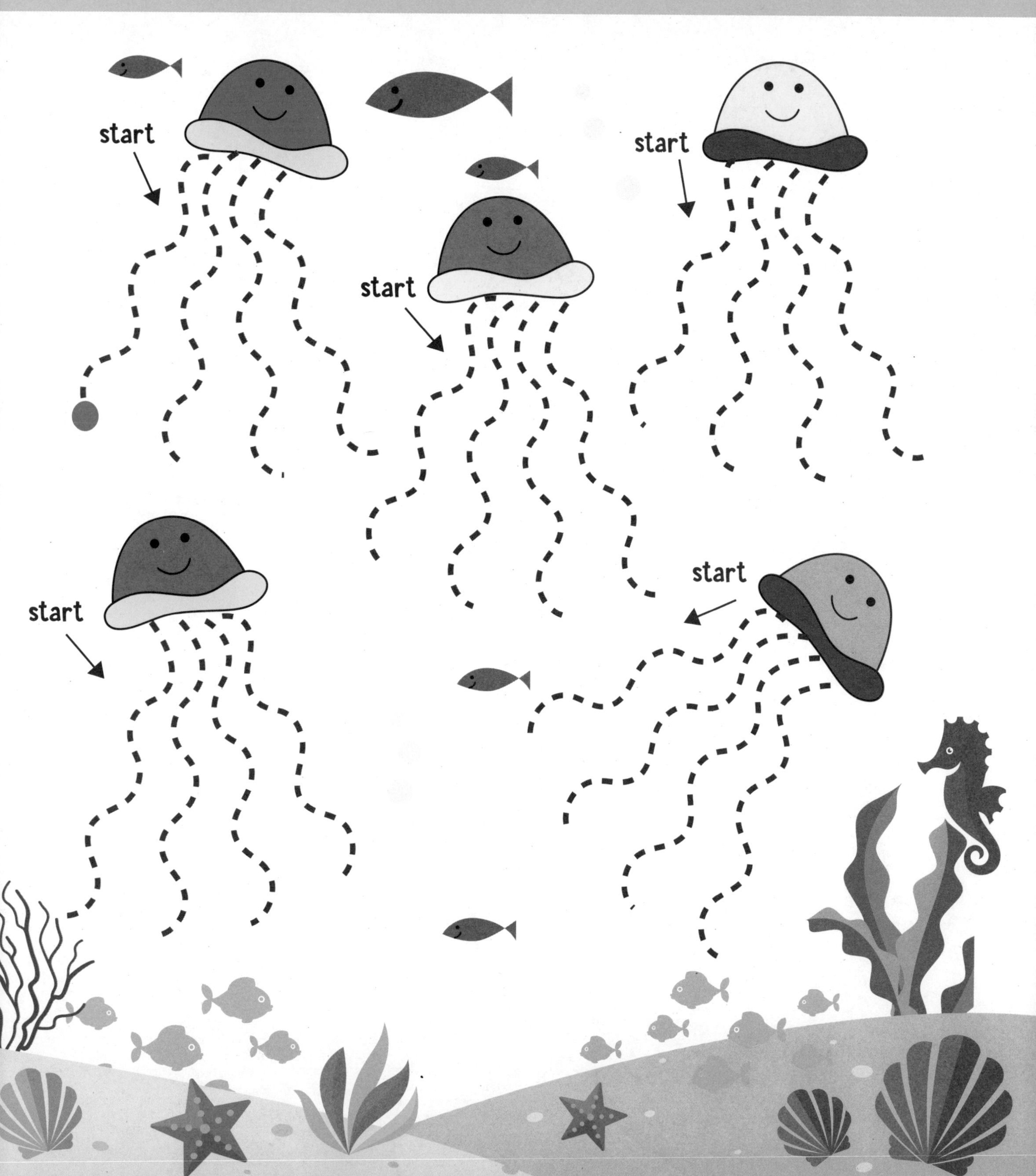

My House

Join the dots from 1 to 10 and color the house.

Ski Path

Trace the path taken by the tourist on the snow peak.

Autumn Foliage

Trace the path of the falling leaves and acorns.

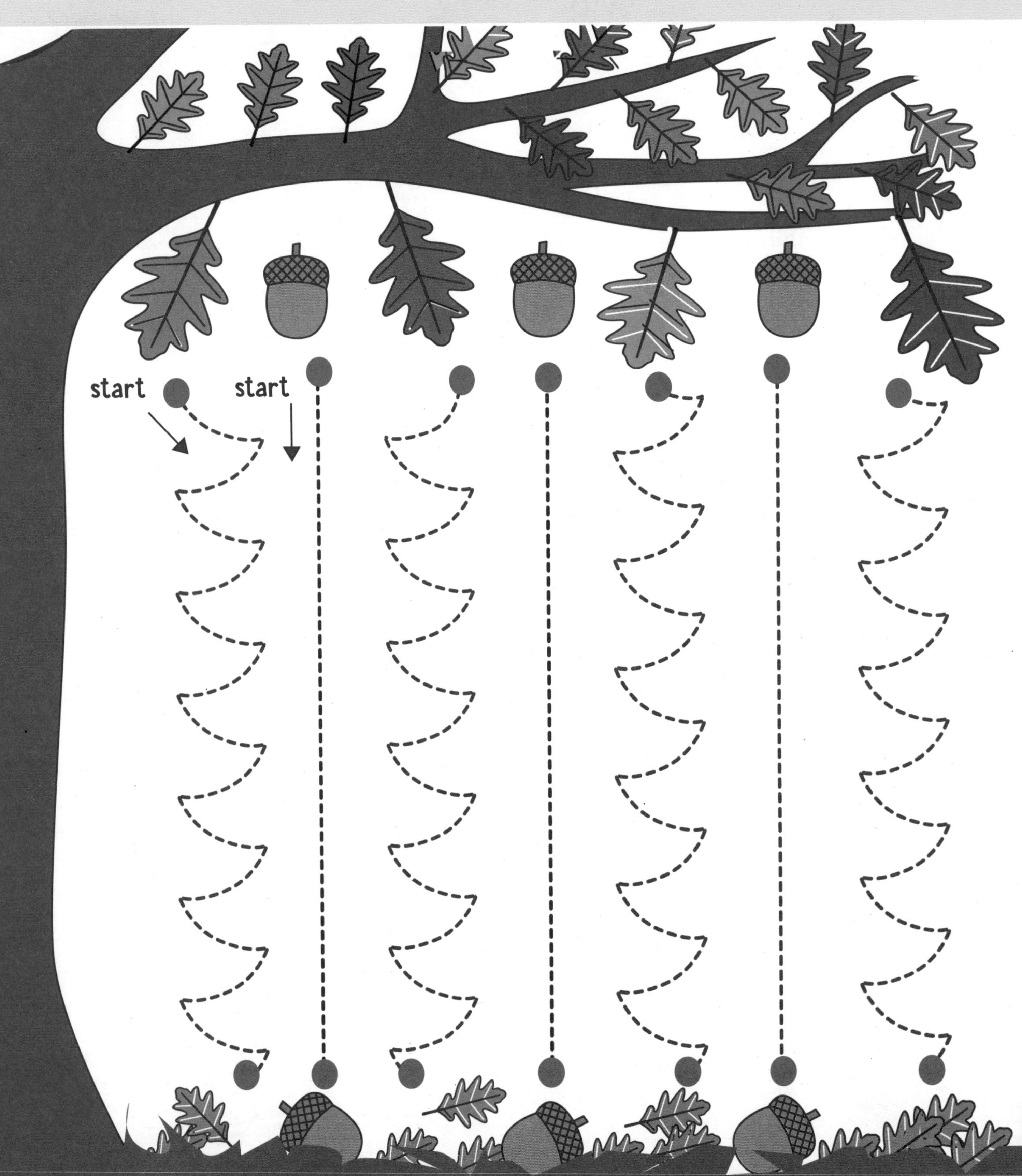

Sunny Day

Trace the dotted lines to complete the sun's rays.

Lines and Vehicles

Trace the lines and match the vehicles.

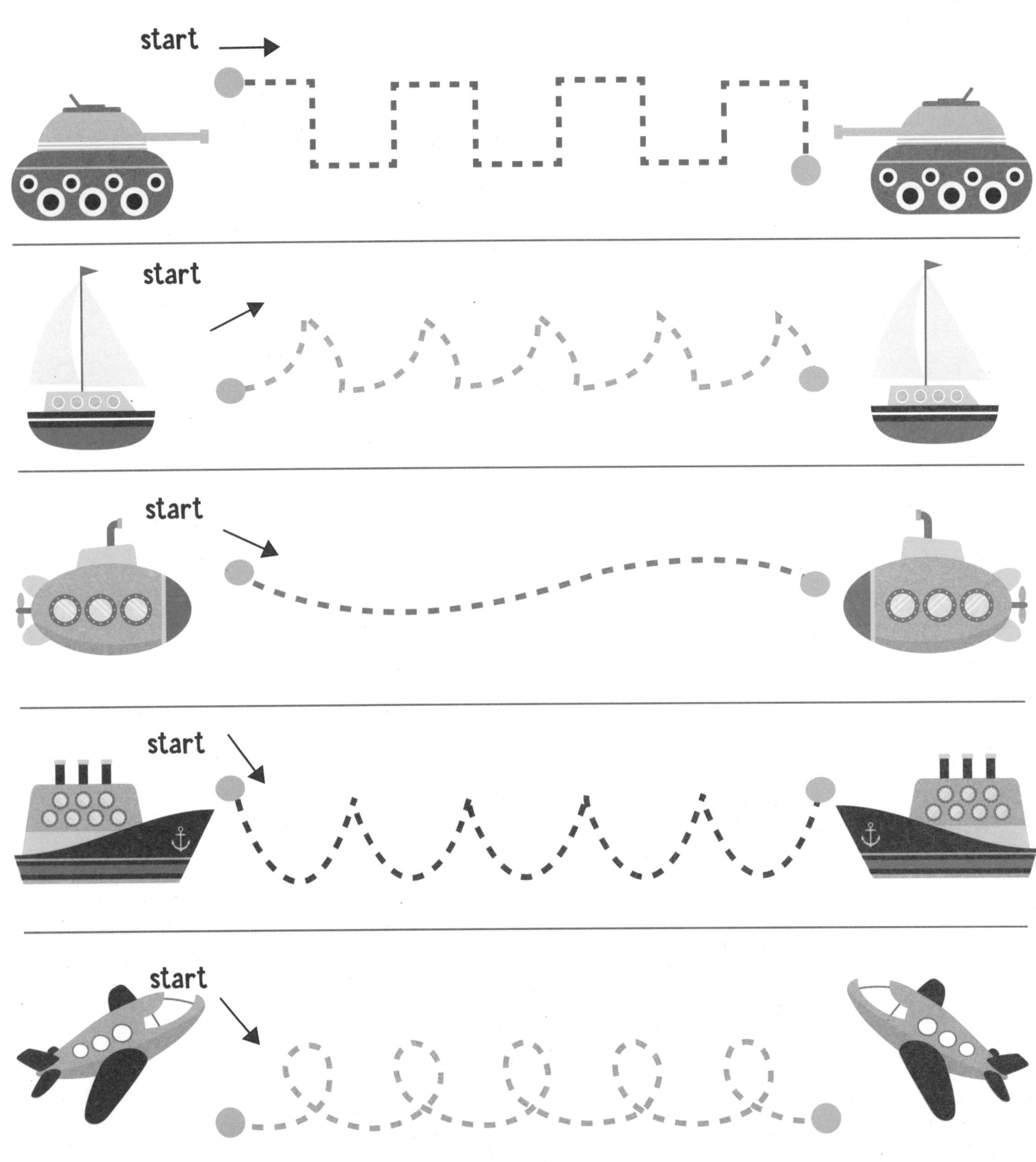

Busy Bees

Trace the lines and help the bees reach the flowers.

Spiral Patterns

Trace the spiral lines and complete the snails.

Candy Color

Trace the spiral lines and color the candies.

Blooming Tulips

Trace the spiral lines and color the tulips.

Join the Dots

Join the dots and complete the butterfly.

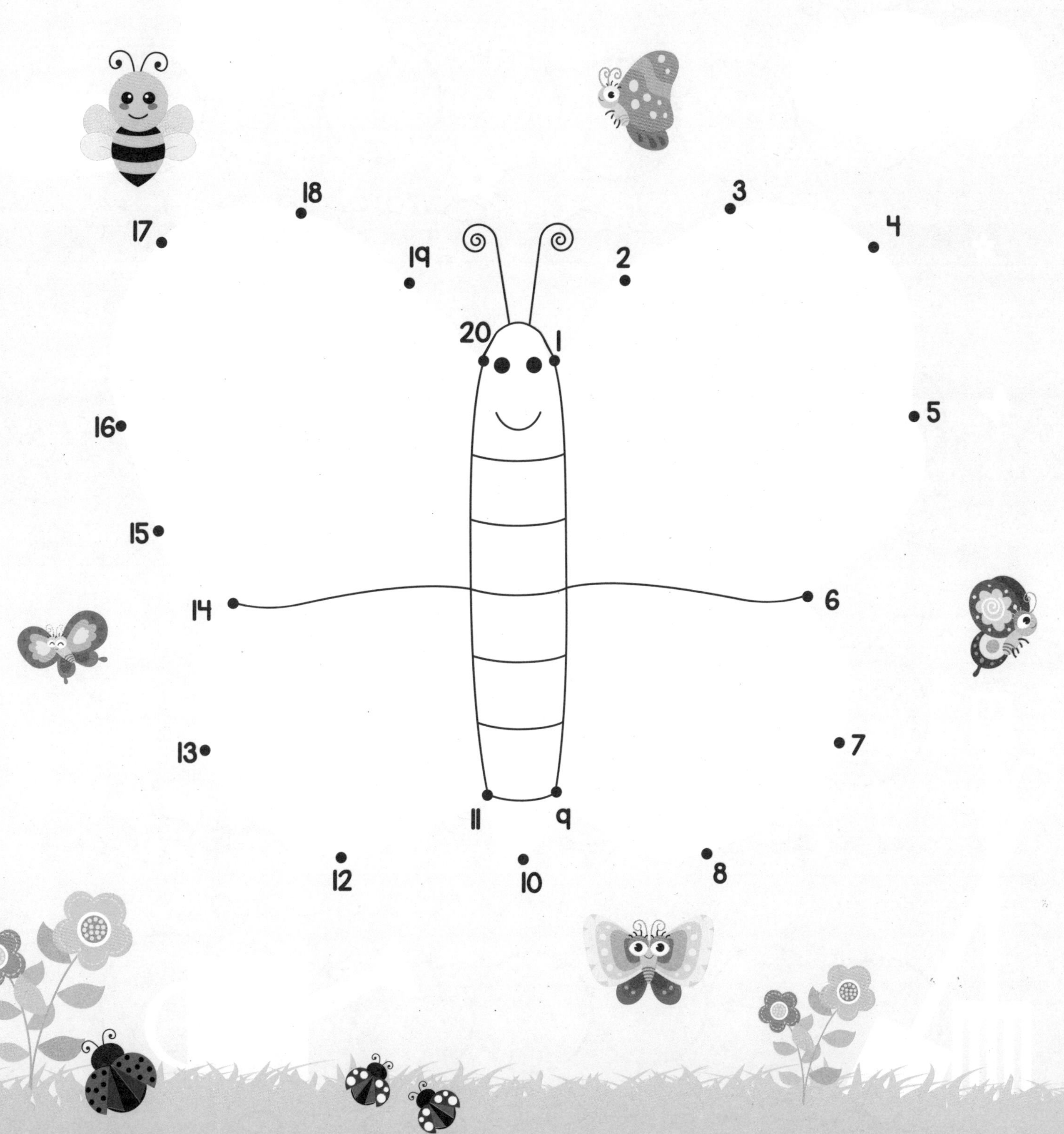

Caterpillars

Trace the circles and complete the caterpillars.

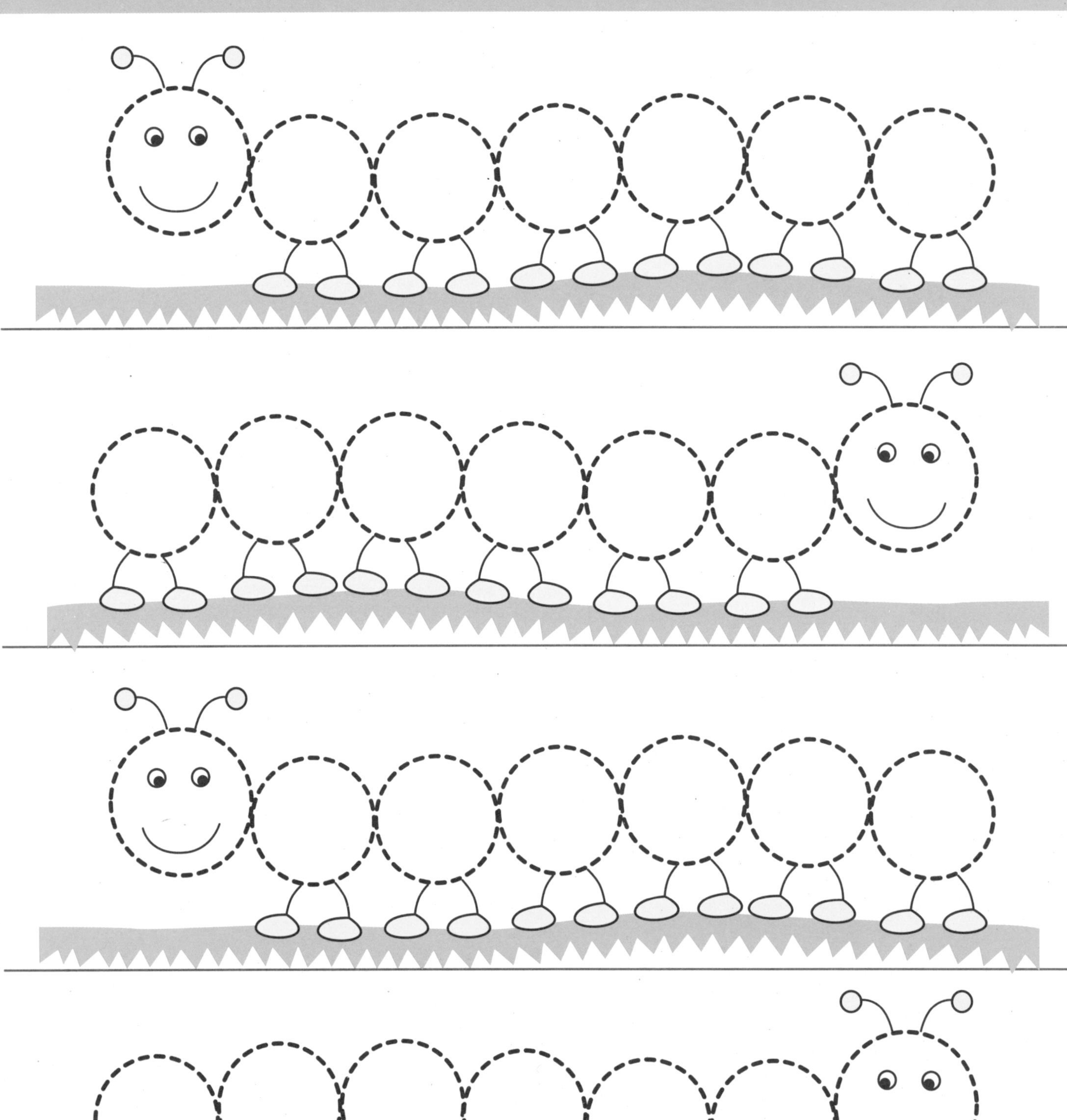

Ladybird

Trace the circles and color the ladybirds.

House and Windows

Trace the square windows and complete the house.

A Colorful Train

Trace the dotted lines and complete the train.

Stars

Trace the dotted lines and color to complete the stars.

Pine Trees

Trace the dotted lines and color to complete the trees.

Basic Shapes

Trace the dotted lines and complete the patterns.

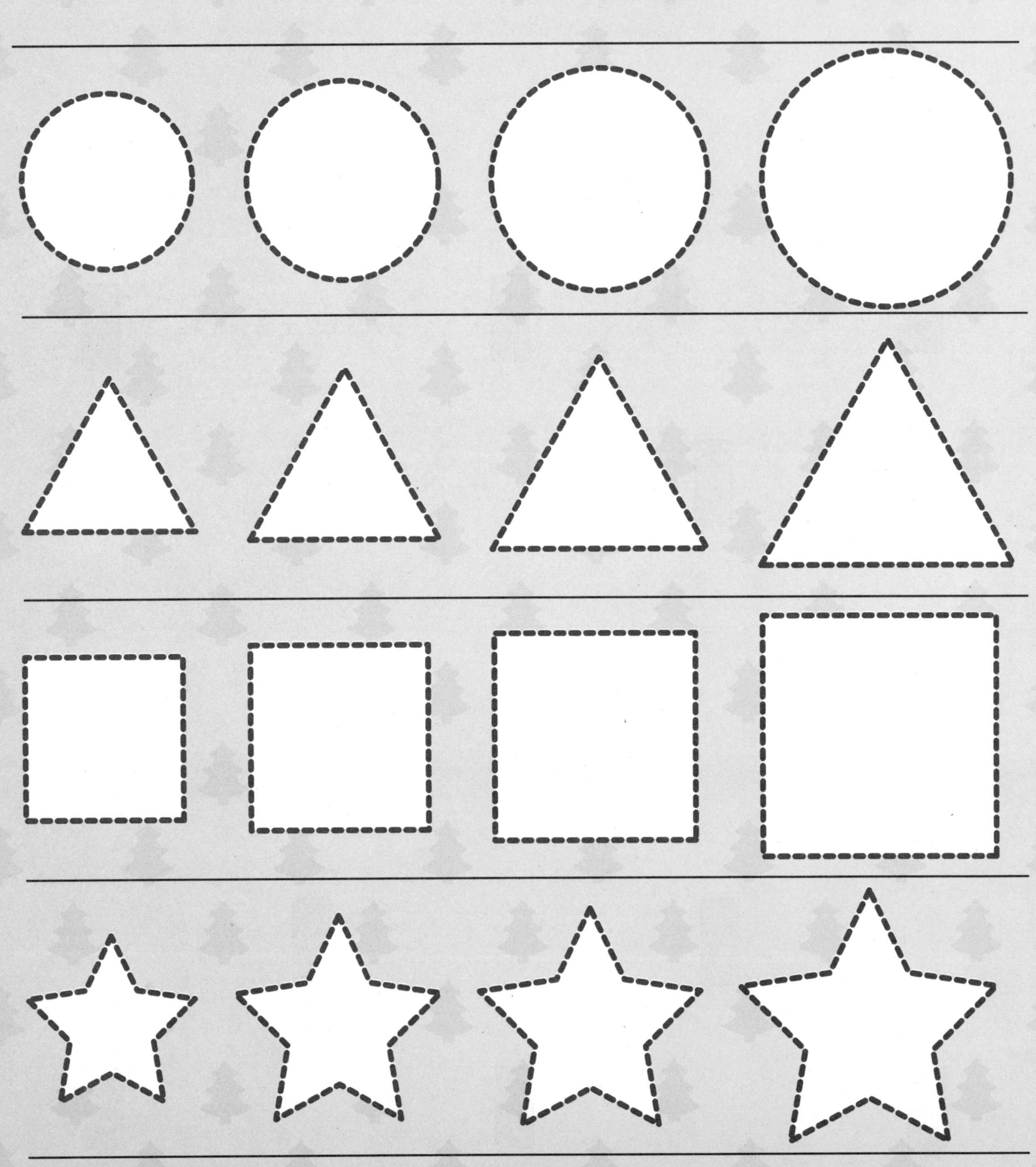

Halloween

Trace the dotted lines and color to complete the Halloween pumpkins.

Butterfly Park

Trace the dotted lines and color to complete the butterflies.

Fish Pond

Trace the dotted lines and color to complete the fish pattern.

Chef's Magic

Trace the dotted lines and complete the pattern.

Smoke Trail

Trace the dotted lines and complete the pattern.

Elephant Bath

Trace the dotted lines and help the elephant take a bath.

Spider Web

Trace the dotted lines and complete the web pattern.

Rainbow Colors

Trace the dotted lines and color the rainbow to complete the picture.

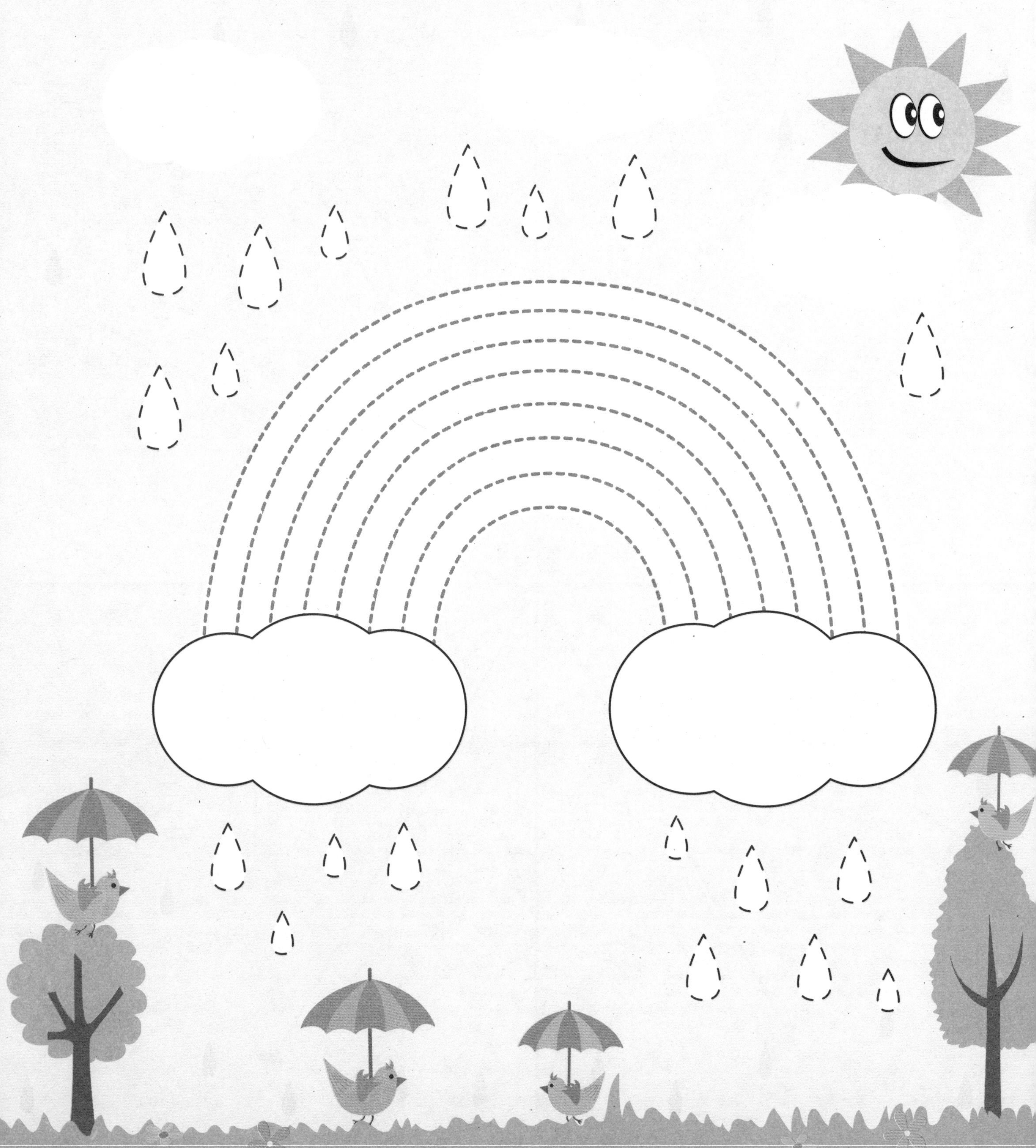

Light House

Trace the dotted lines to complete the pattern.

Merry Christmas!

Trace the dotted lines and color the stocking to complete the pattern.

Christmas Tree

Trace the dotted lines and color the tree.

Birthday Cake

Trace the dotted lines and color the candles to complete the lovely cake.

Yummy Ice Cream

Trace the dotted lines and color the ice cream to complete the tasty treat.

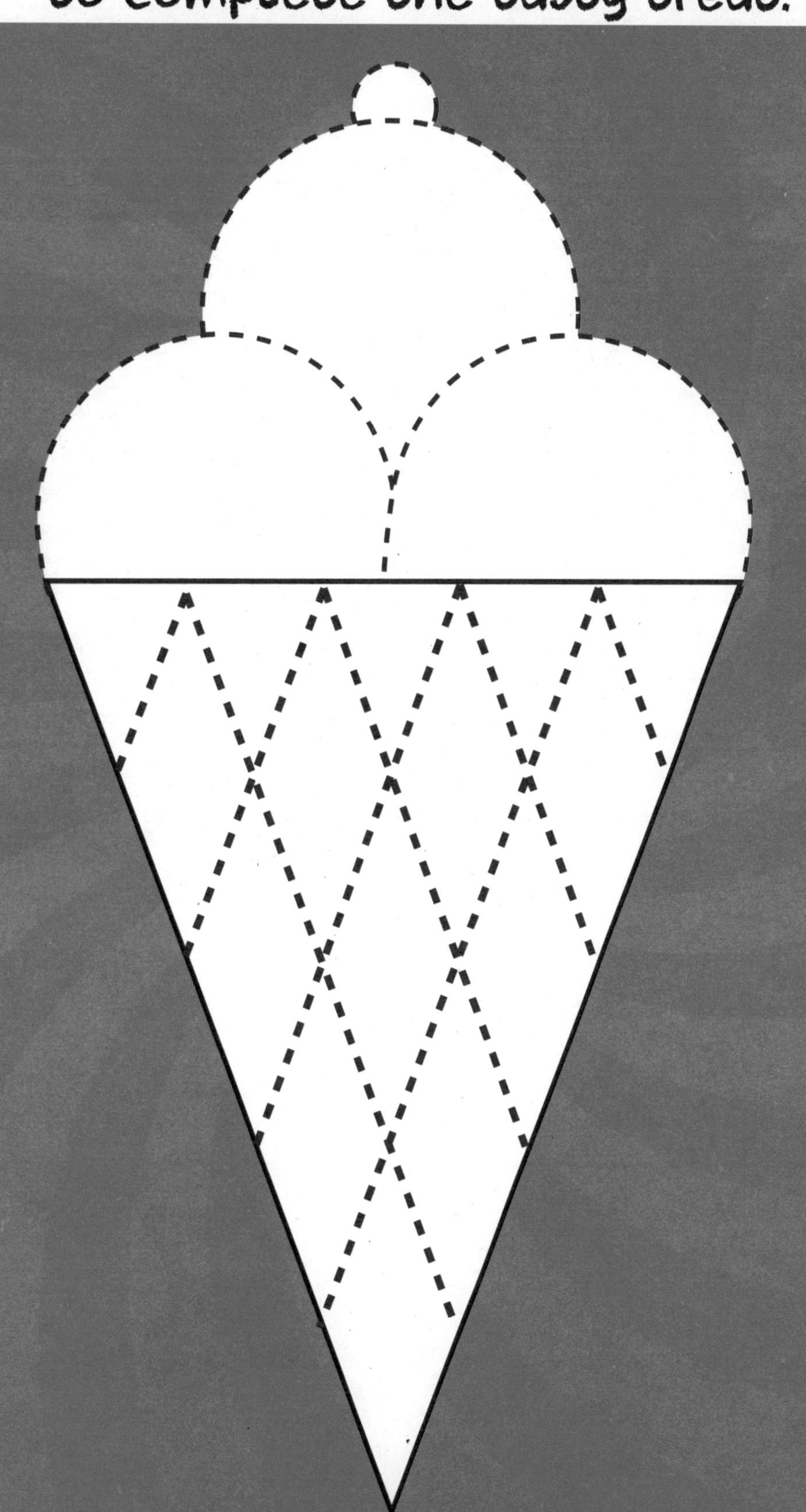

Emergency Helpers

Help the emergency helpers reach their vehicles.

Travel Buddies

Help the travel buddies reach their vehicles.

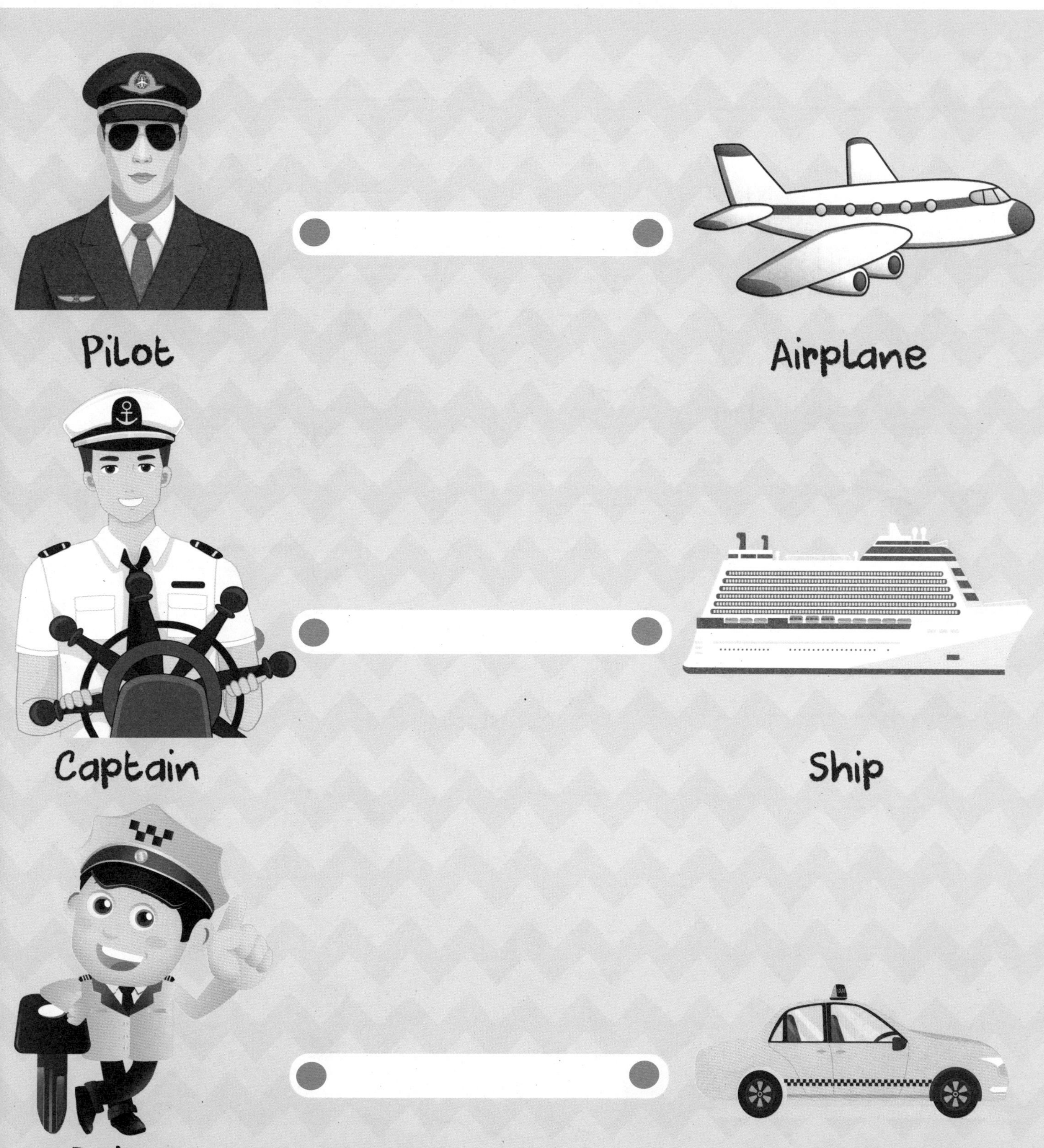

Balloon Race

Trace the lines on the hot air balloons and complete the picture.

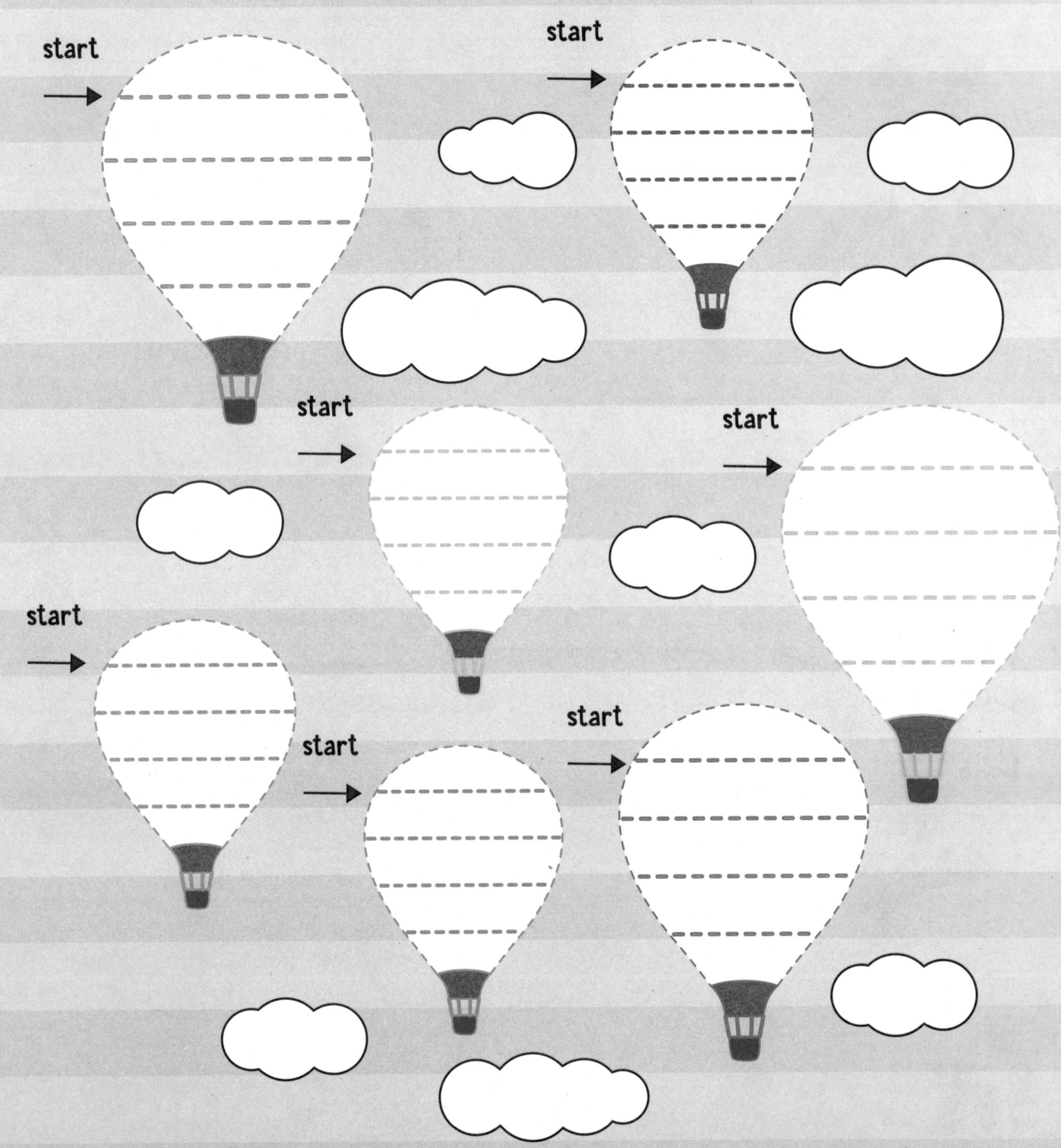

Balloon Strings

Trace the balloon strings and complete the picture.

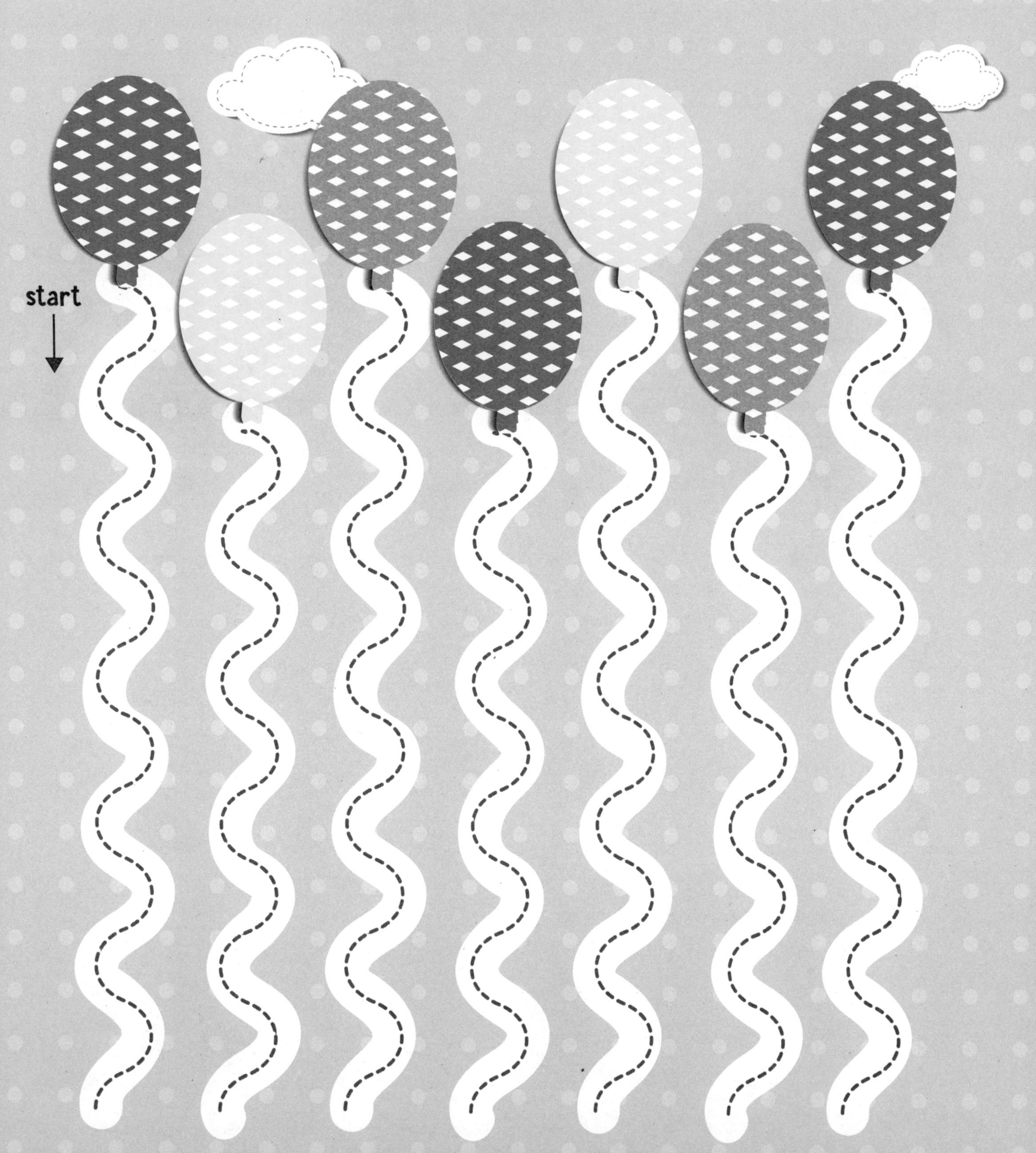

A Winding Way

Help the pirate find treasure by taking the correct path.

My First Book Of Patterns

Capital Letters

With Animal Coloring and Activity Pages

A for ALLigator

Color the Letter A and the ALLIGATOR brightly.

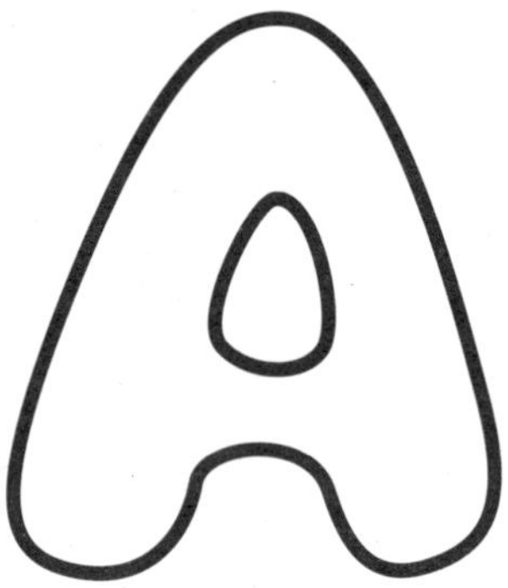

Alligator

Trace the Letter.

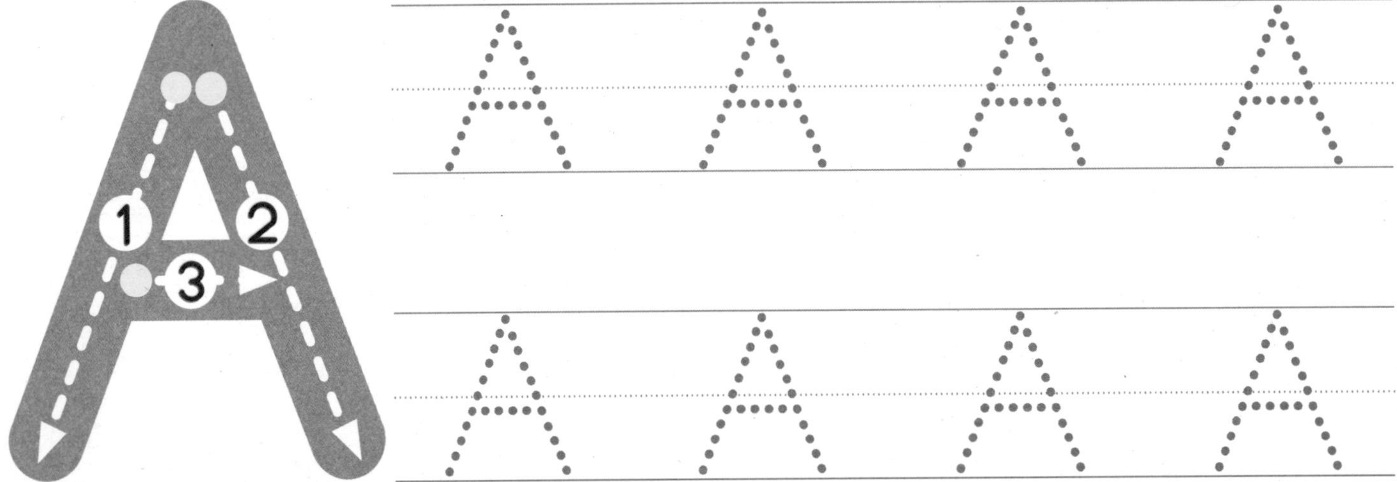

B for Bear

Color the letter B and the BEAR brightly.

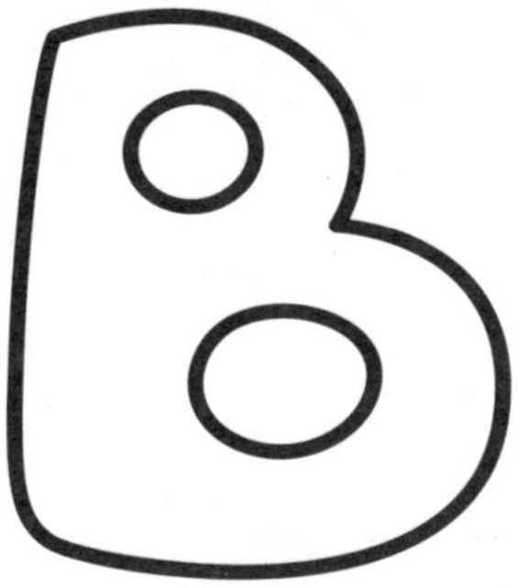

Bear

Trace the letter.

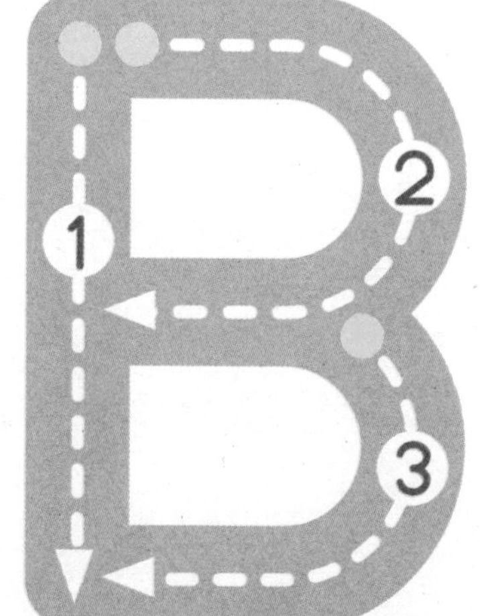

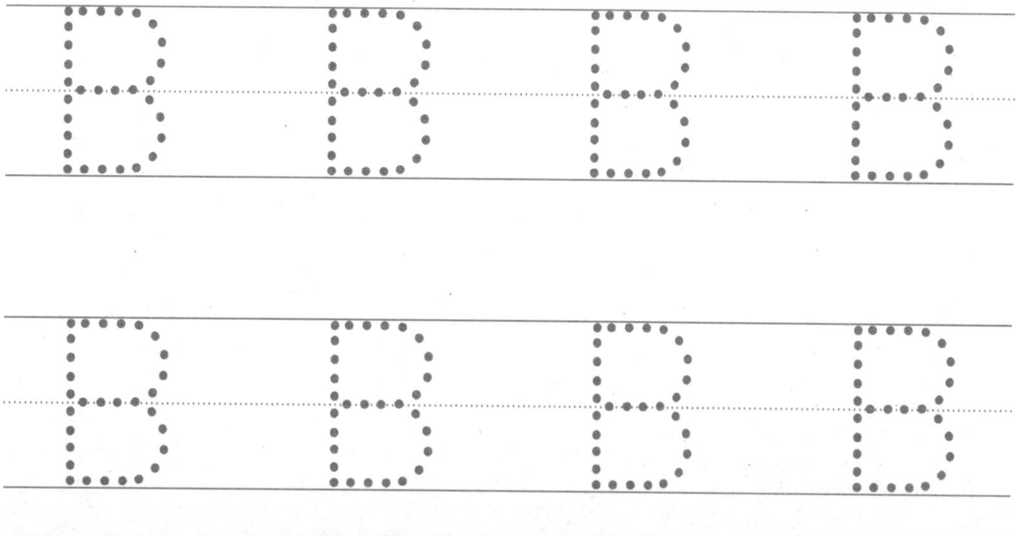

B B B B

B B B B

C for Cat

Color the Letter C and the CAT brightly.

Trace the Letter.

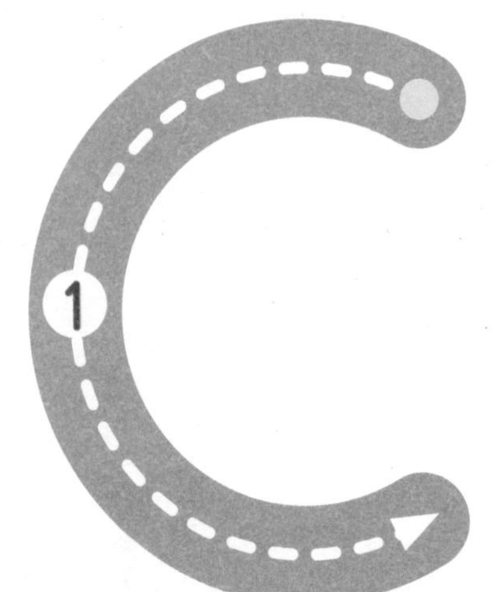

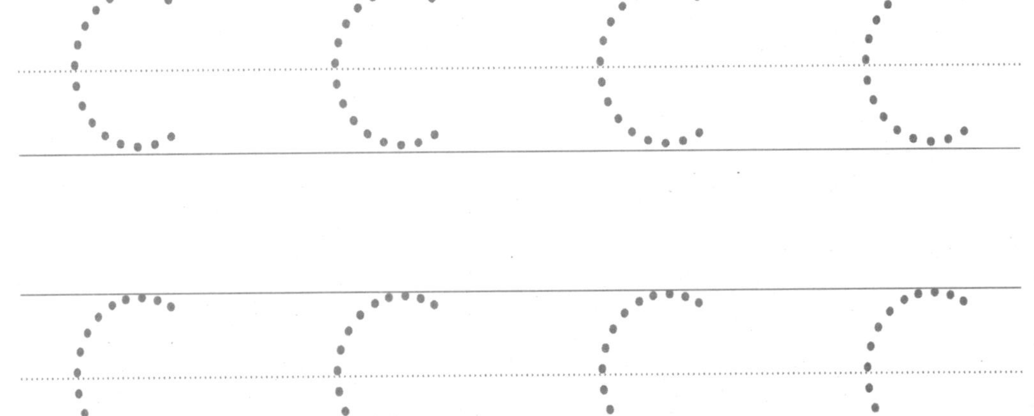

D for Dog

Color the Letter D and the DOG brightly.

D

Dog

Trace the Letter.

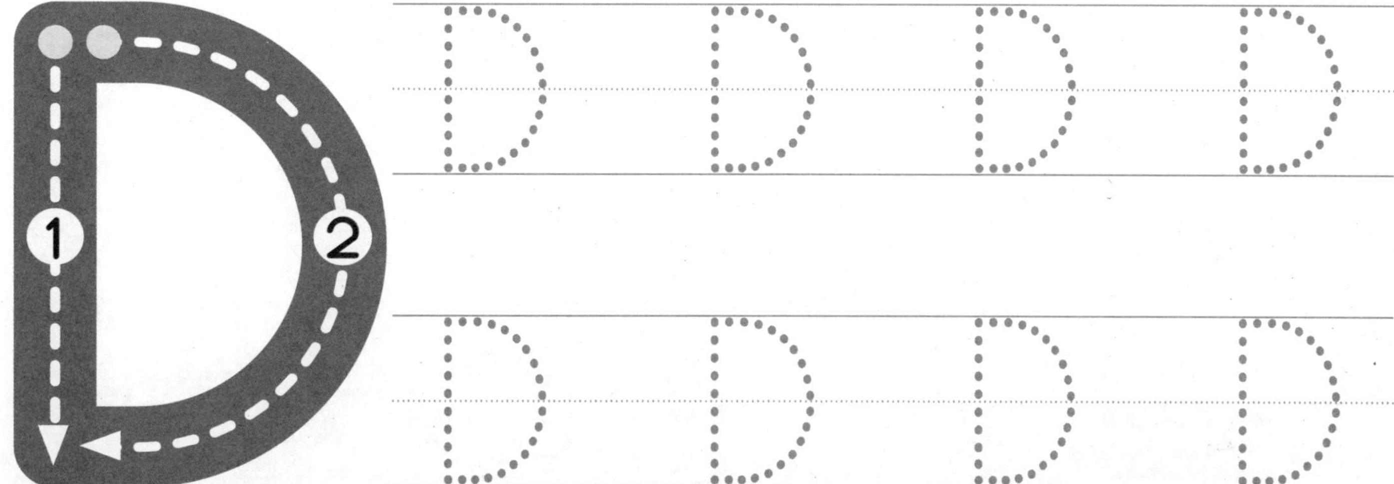

E for Elephant

Color the letter E and the ELEPHANT brightly.

Elephant

Trace the letter.

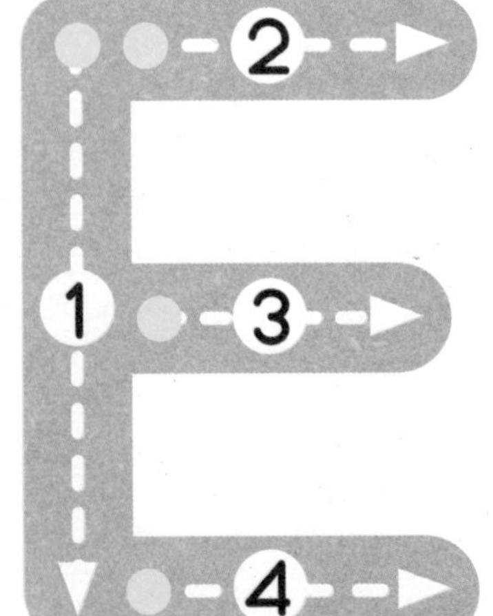

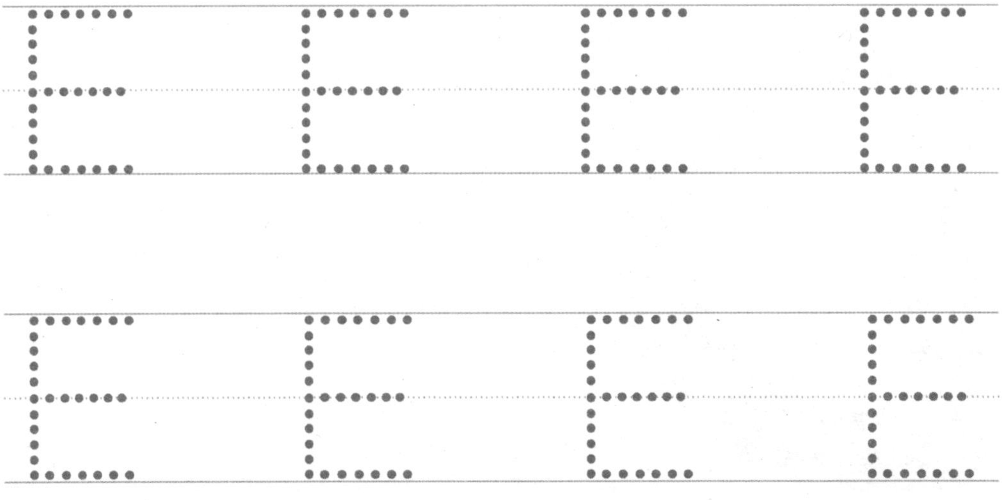

Find the First Letter!

Circle the beginning letter of each picture.

E A B

C E B

D A E

A D C

Draw a Circle around the pictures whose name begins with the given letter.

Draw a line from each letter to the picture whose name begins with that letter.

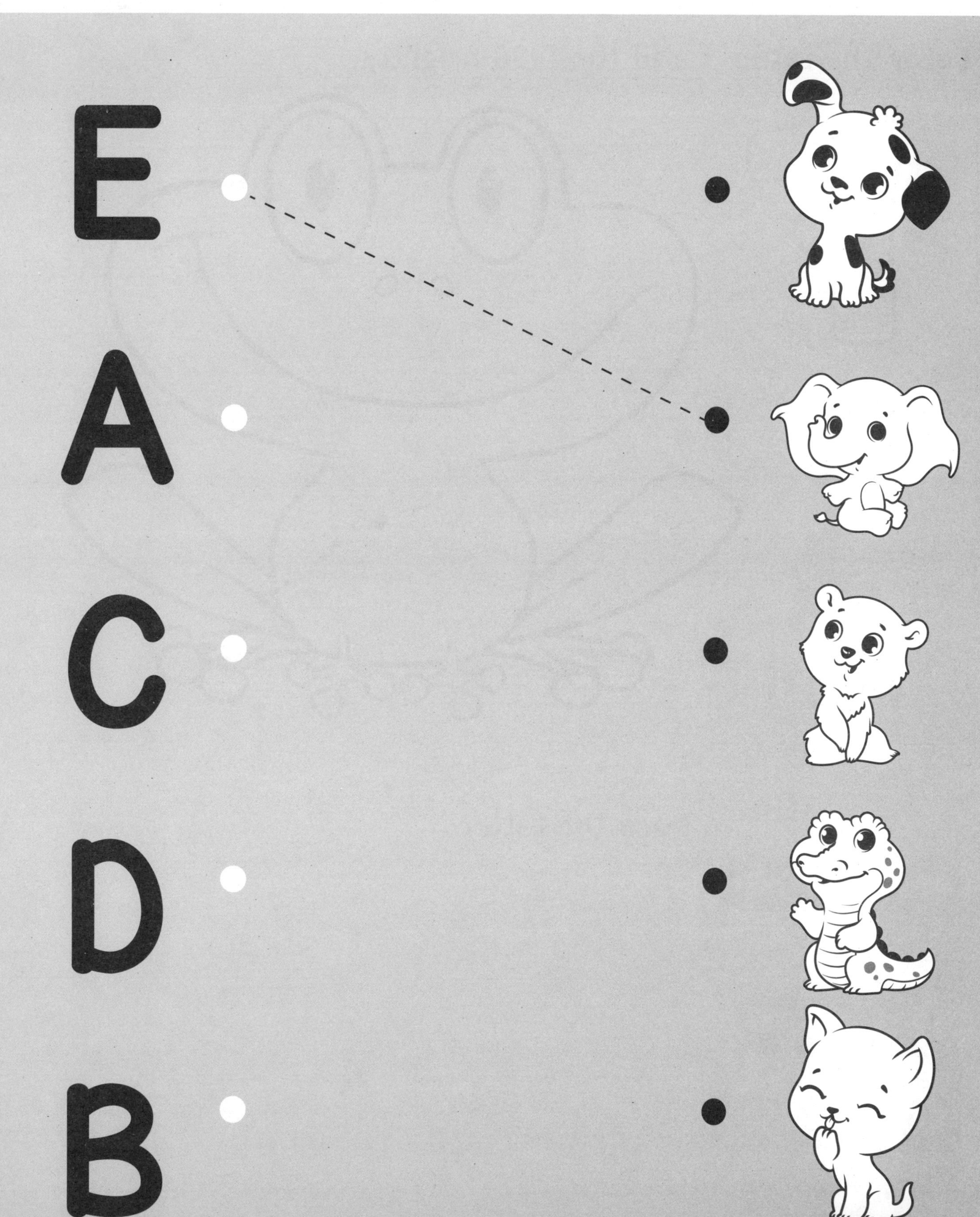

F for Frog

Color the letter f and the FROG brightly.

Frog

Trace the letter.

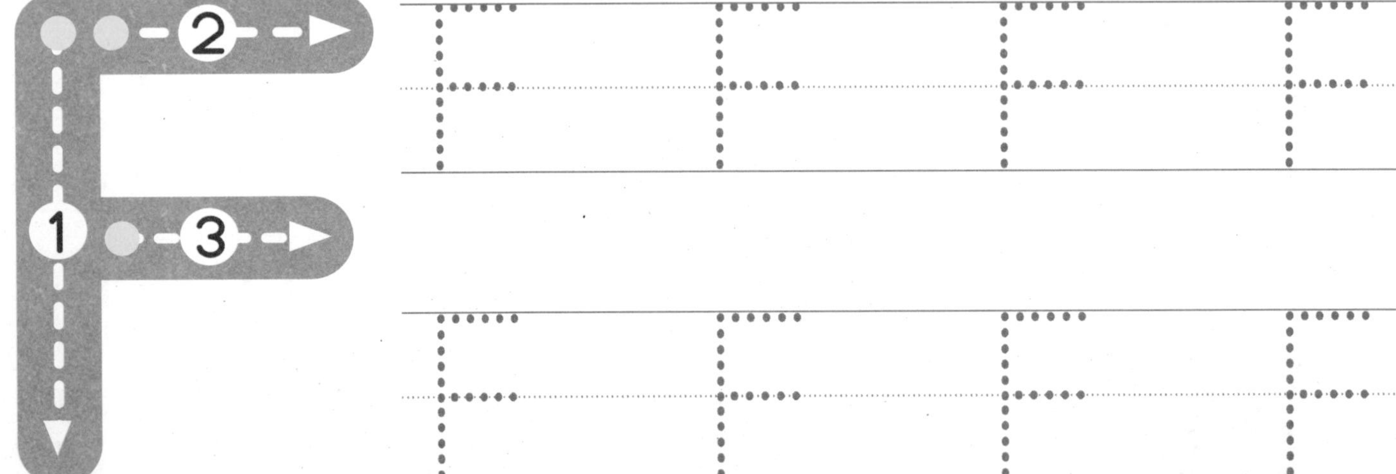

G for Giraffe

Color the Letter G and the GIRAFFE brightly.

Giraffe

Trace the Letter.

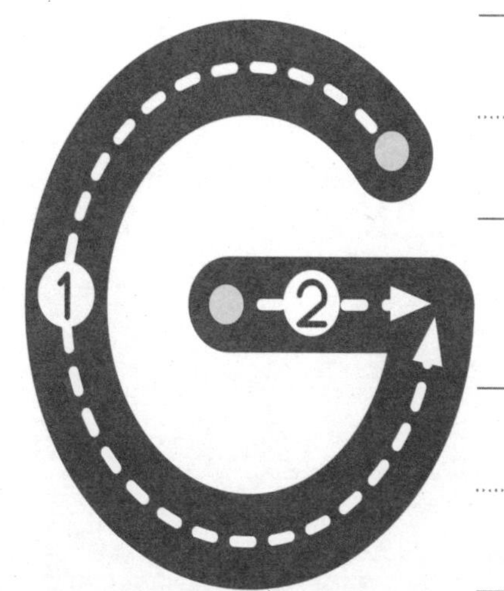

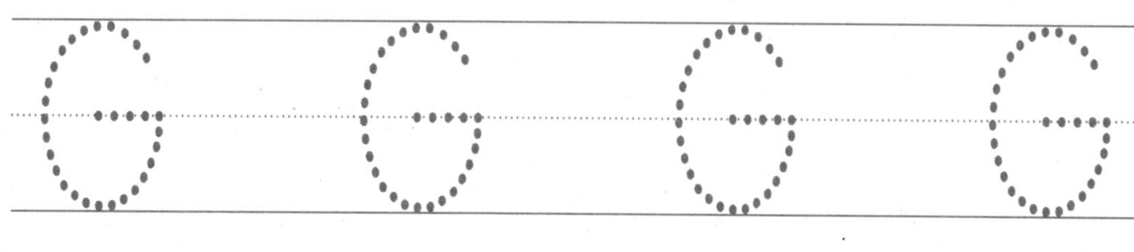

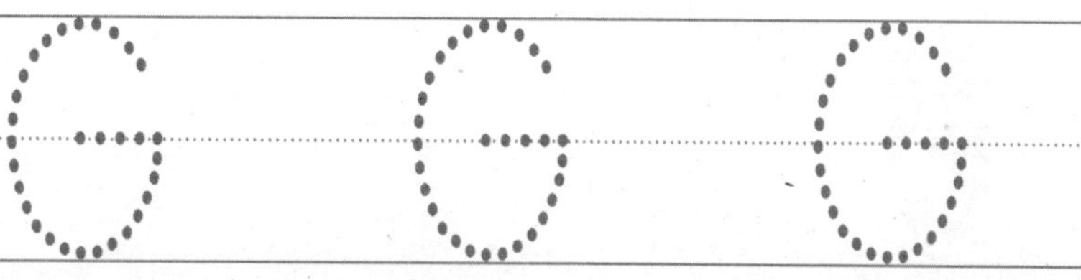

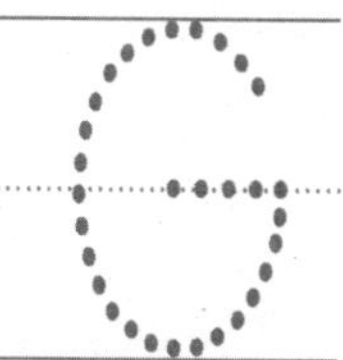

H for Horse

Color the Letter H and the HORSE brightly.

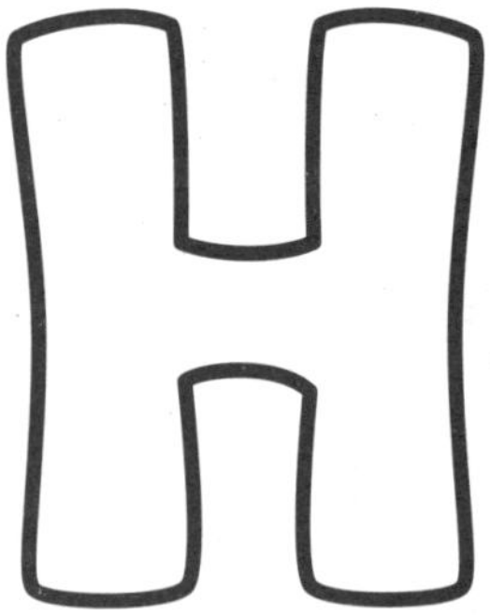

Horse

Trace the Letter.

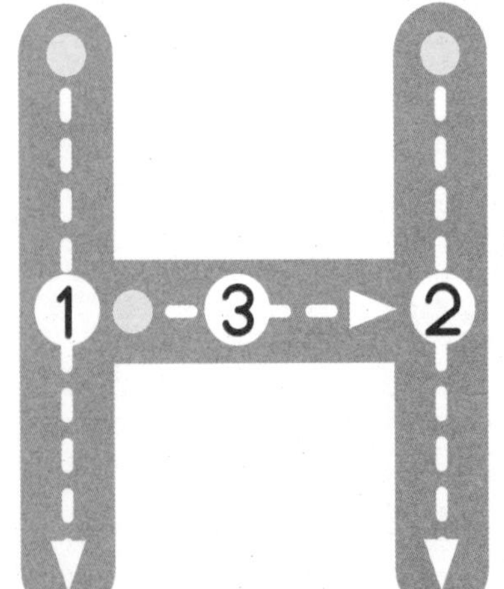

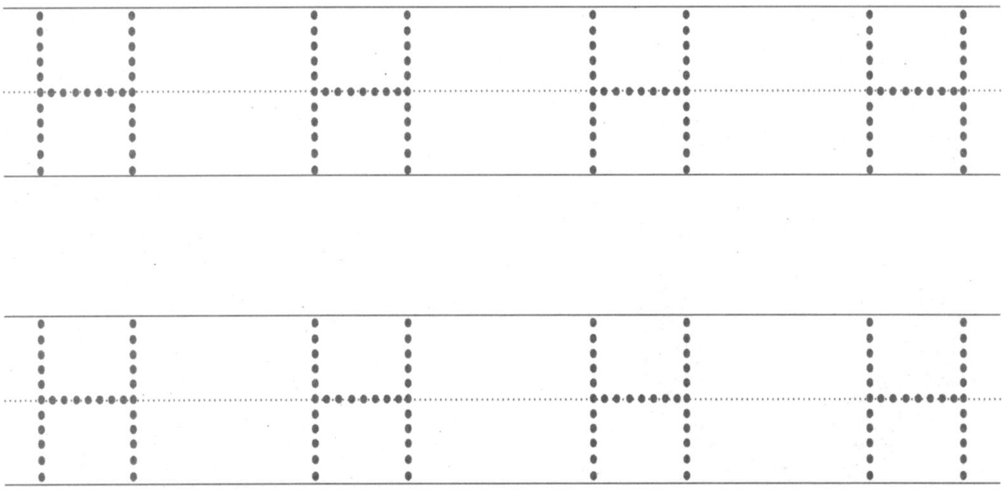

I for Iguana

Color the Letter I and the IGUANA brightly.

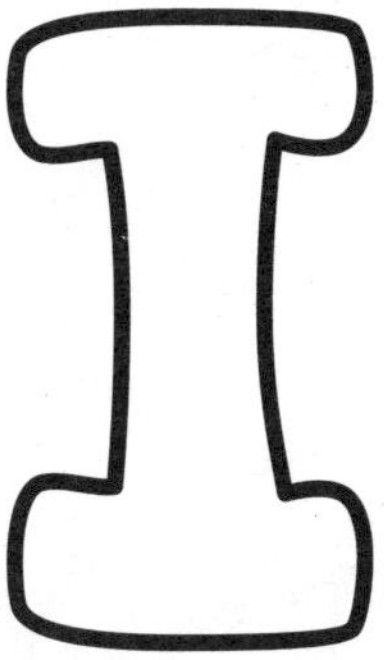

Iguana

Trace the Letter.

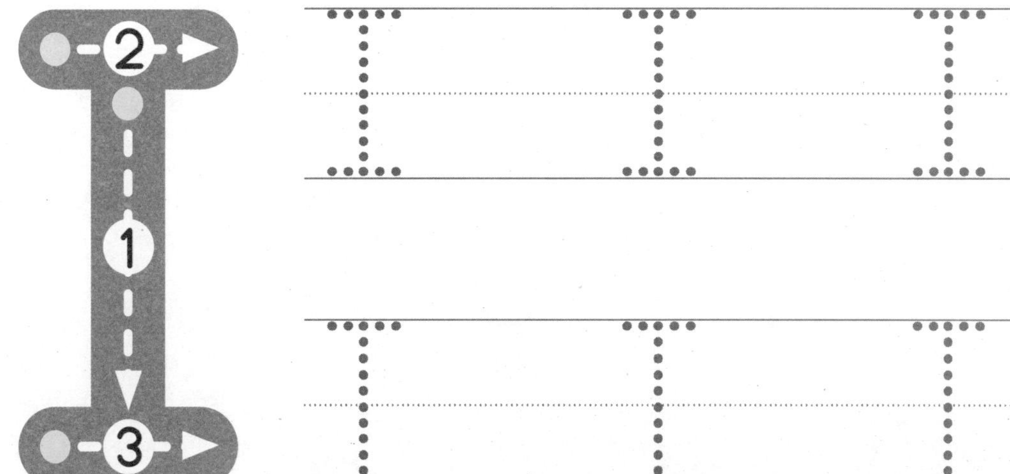

J for Jellyfish

Color the letter J and the JELLYFISH brightly.

Jellyfish

Trace the letter.

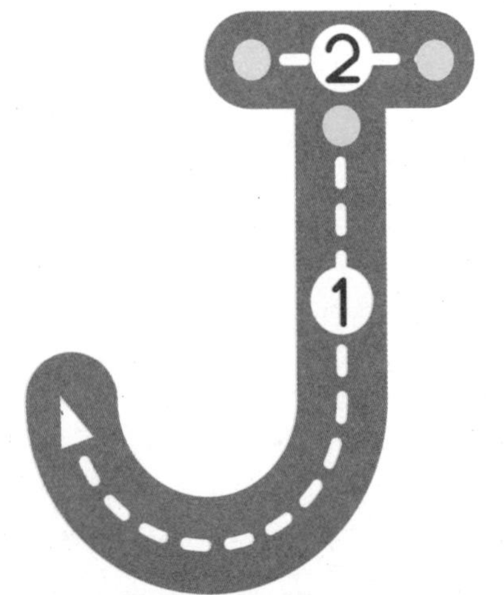

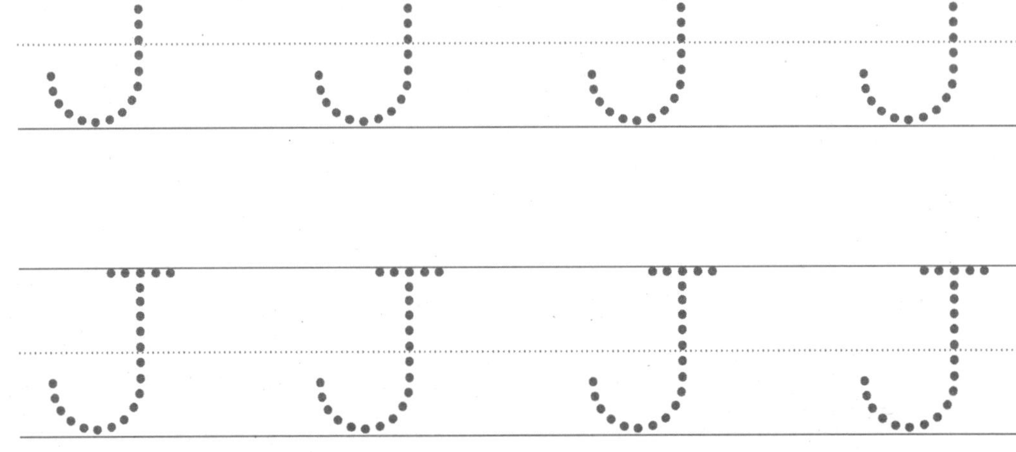

Find the First Letter!

Circle the beginning letter of each picture.

G J I

F H G

I G J

H J G

Draw a Circle around the pictures whose name begins with the given letter.

Draw a line from each letter to the picture whose name begins with that letter.

Color the letter K and the KOALA brightly.

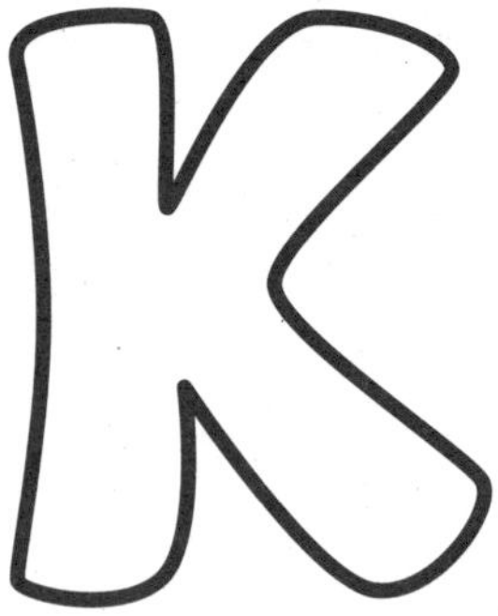

K

Koala

Trace the letter.

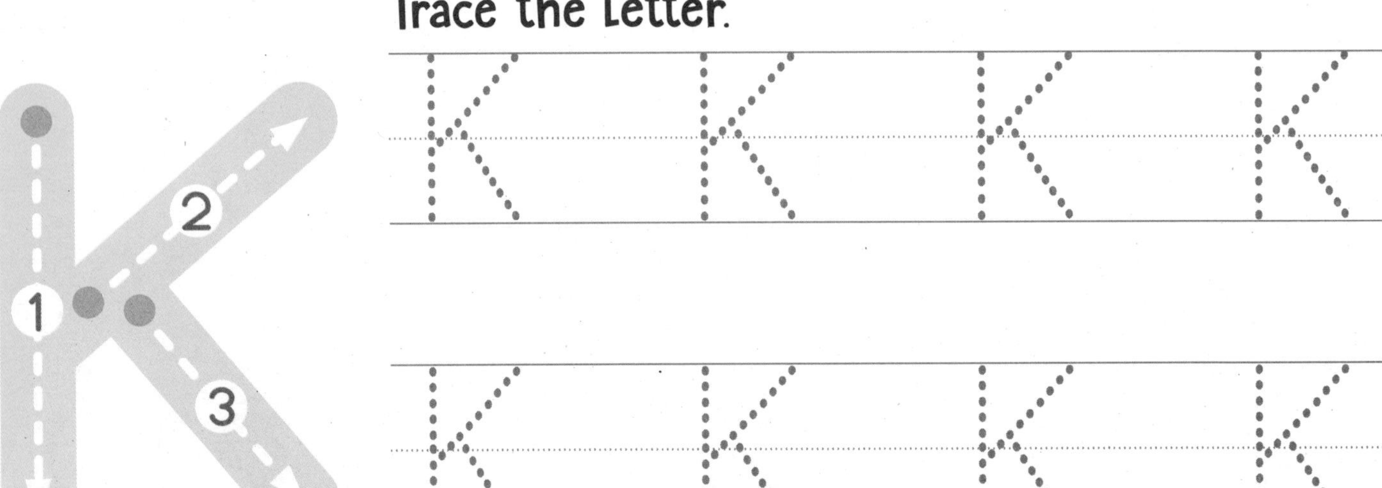

L for Lion

Color the Letter L and the LION brightly.

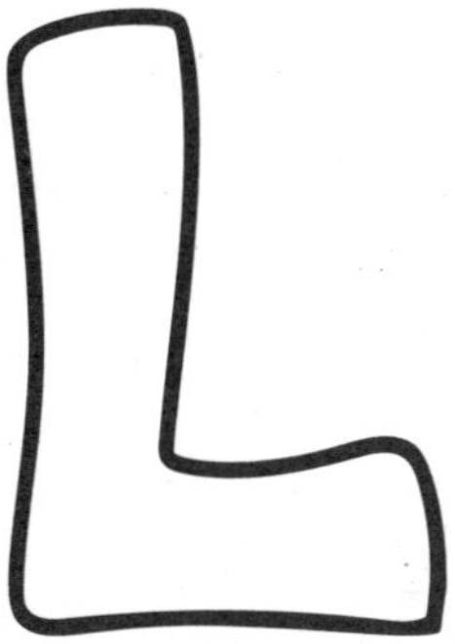

Lion

Trace the Letter.

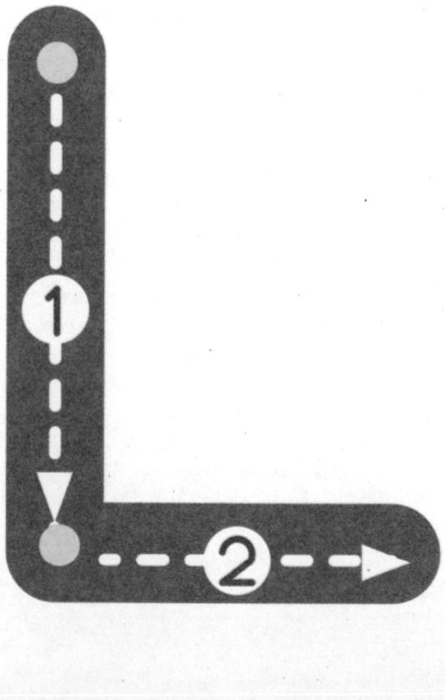

1

2

Color the letter M and the MONKEY brightly.

Trace the letter.

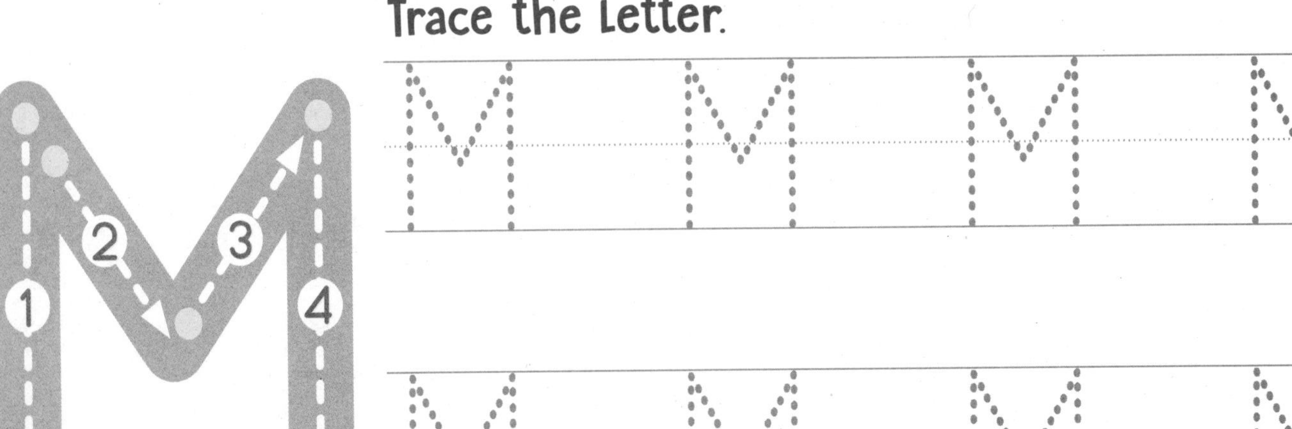

N for Nightingale

Color the Letter N and the NIGHTINGALE brightly.

N

Nightingale

Trace the Letter.

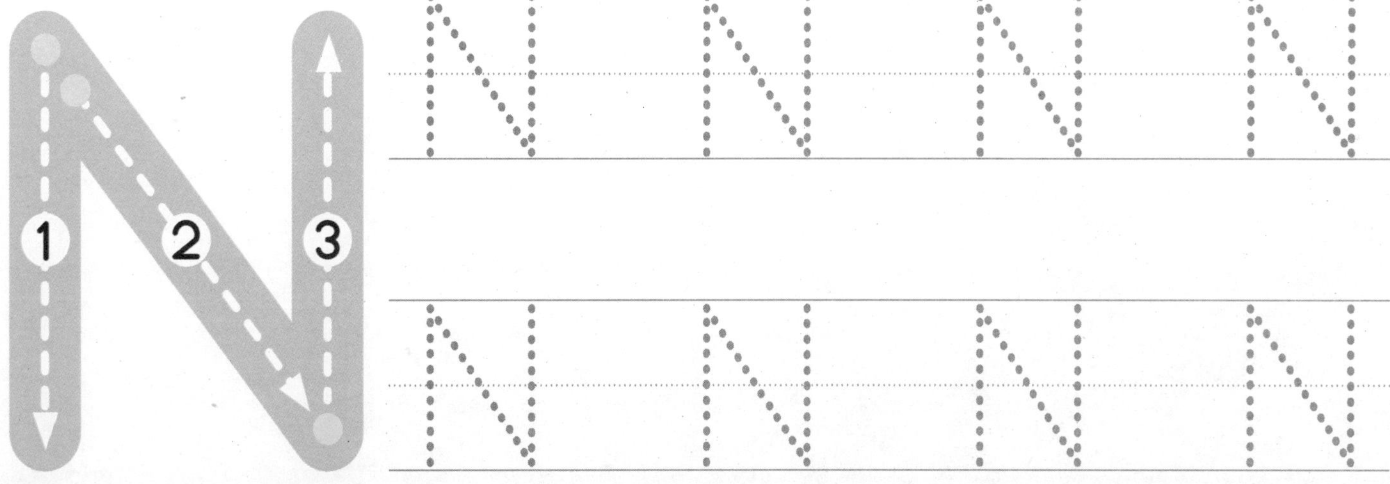

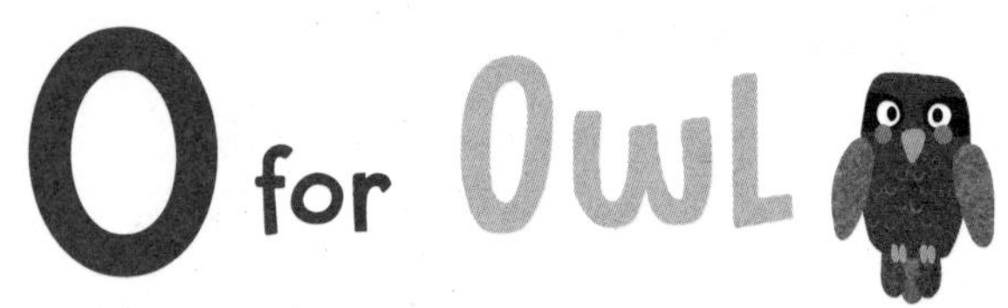
O for OWL

Color the Letter O and the OWL brightly.

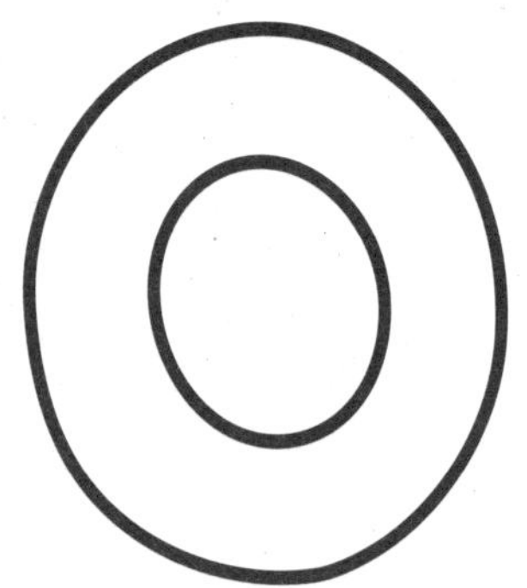

Owl

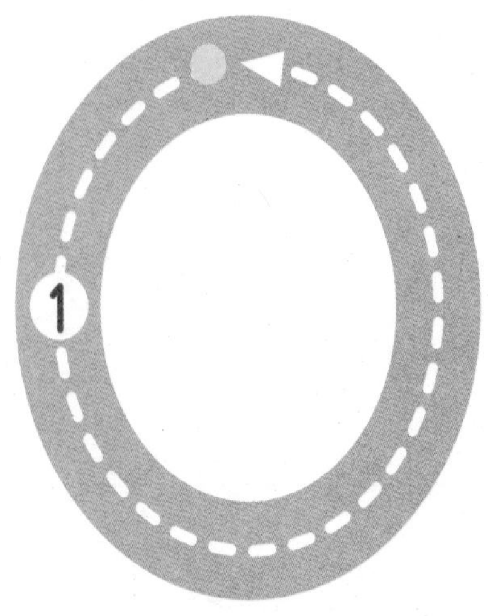
1

Trace the Letter.

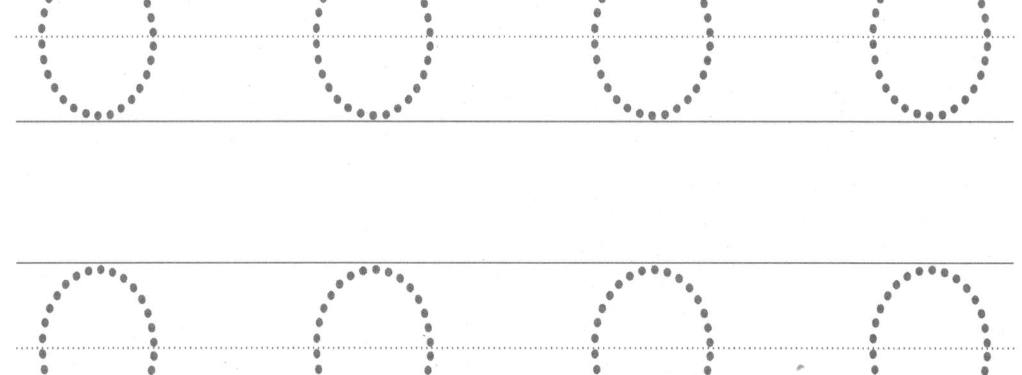

Find the First Letter!

Circle the beginning letter of each picture.

K M O

L N M

N M O

N L K

Draw a Circle around the pictures whose name begins with the given letter.

Draw a line from each letter to the picture whose name begins with that letter.

Color the Letter P and the PARROT brightly.

Parrot

Trace the Letter.

Color the Letter Q and the QUEEN BEE brightly.

Queen Bee

Trace the Letter.

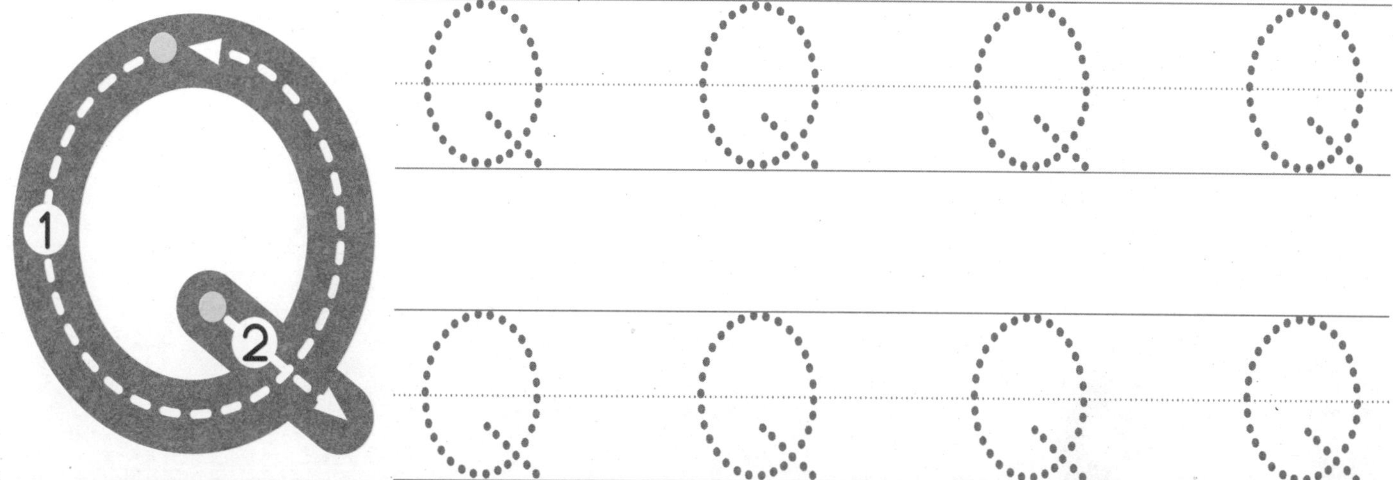

R for Rhinoceros

Color the Letter R and the RHINOCEROS brightly.

Rhinoceros

Trace the Letter.

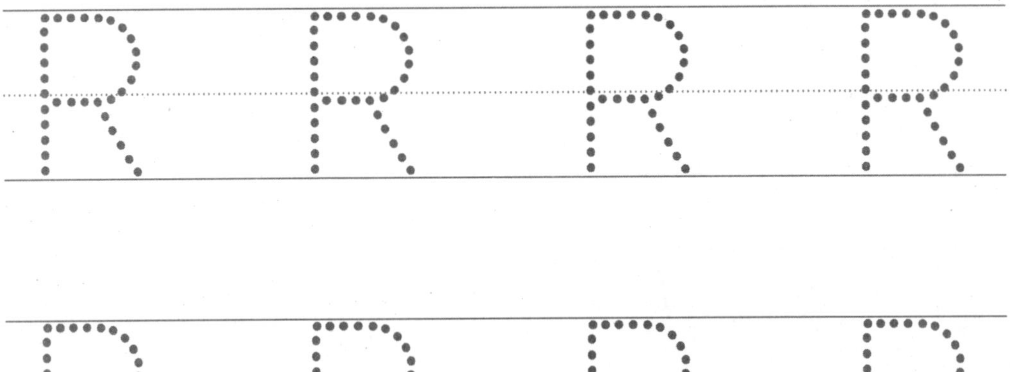

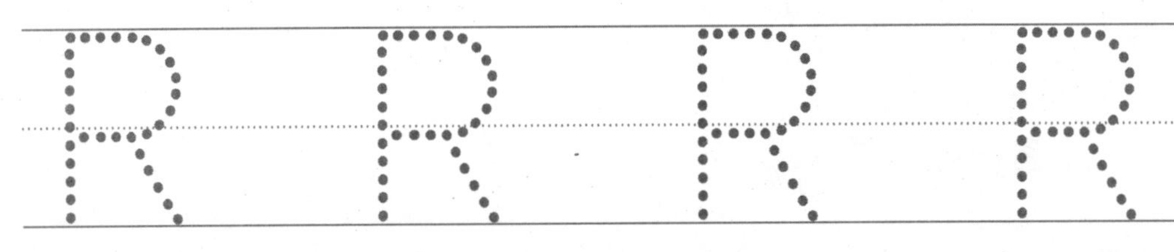

S for Squirrel

Color the Letter S and the SQUIRREL brightly.

S

Squirrel

Trace the Letter.

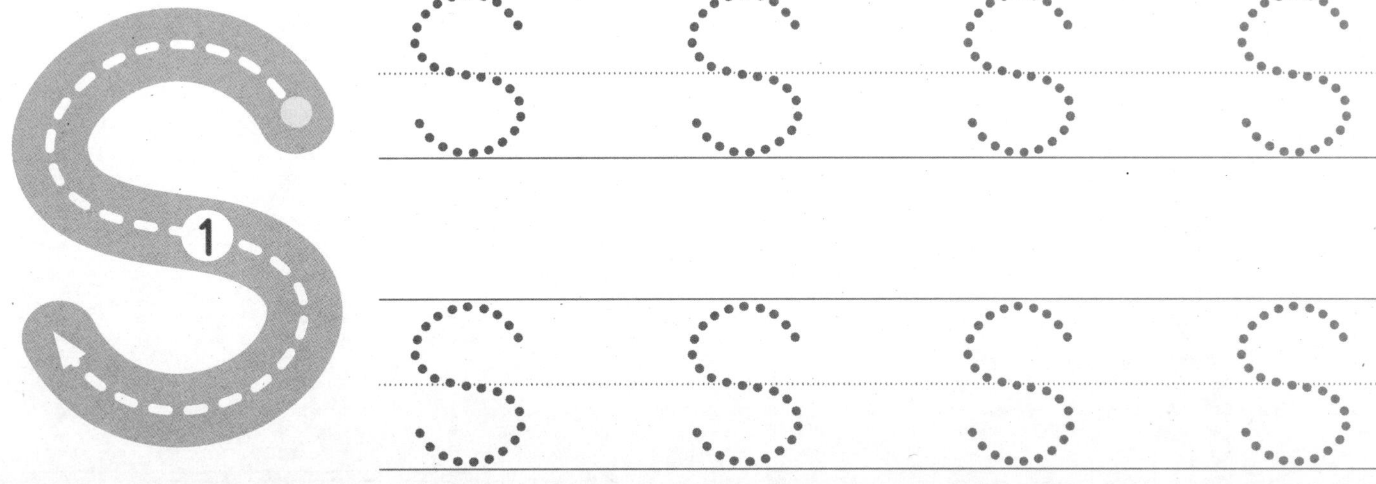

T for Tortoise

Color the Letter T and the TORTOISE brightly.

Tortoise

Trace the Letter.

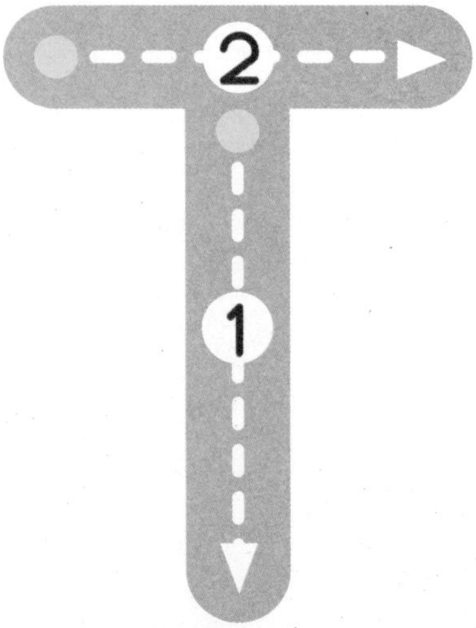

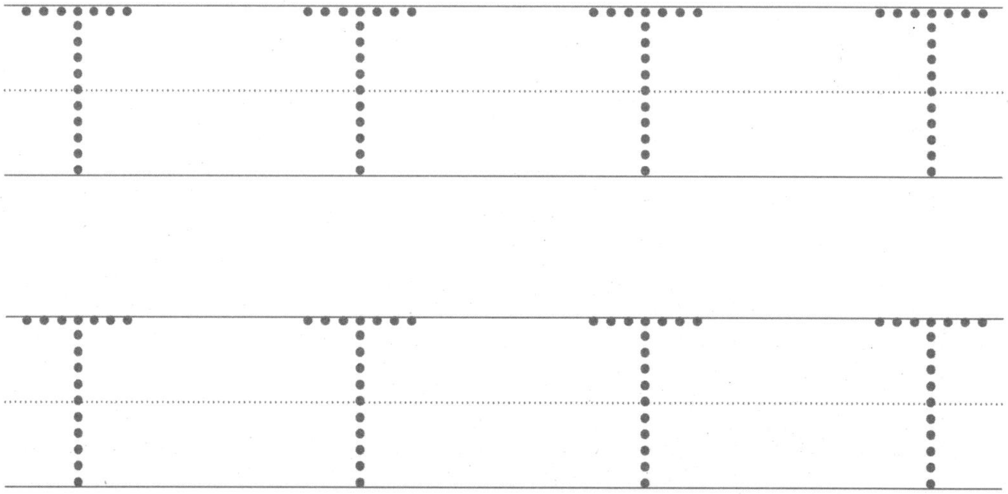

Find the First Letter!

Circle the beginning letter of each picture.

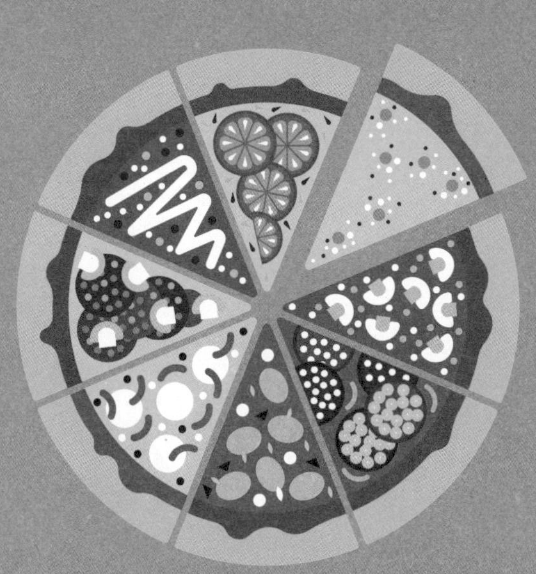

P R S

Q S R

T R S

S P Q

Draw a circle around the pictures whose name begins with the given letter.

Draw a line from each letter to the picture whose name begins with that letter.

U for Unicorn

Color the Letter U and the UNICORN brightly.

u

Unicorn

Trace the Letter.

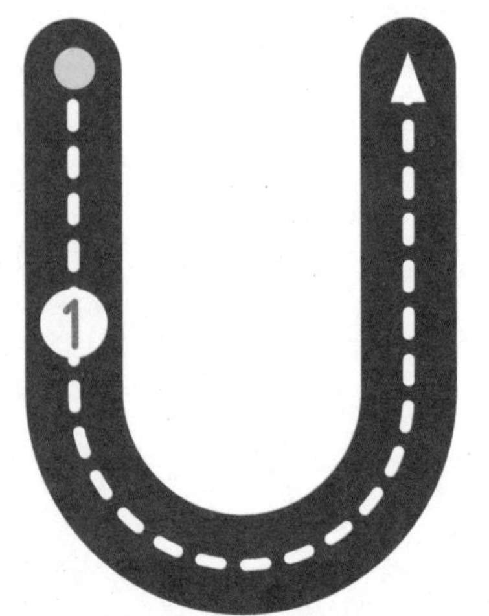

V for Vulture

Color the letter V and the VULTURE brightly.

V

Vulture

Trace the Letter.

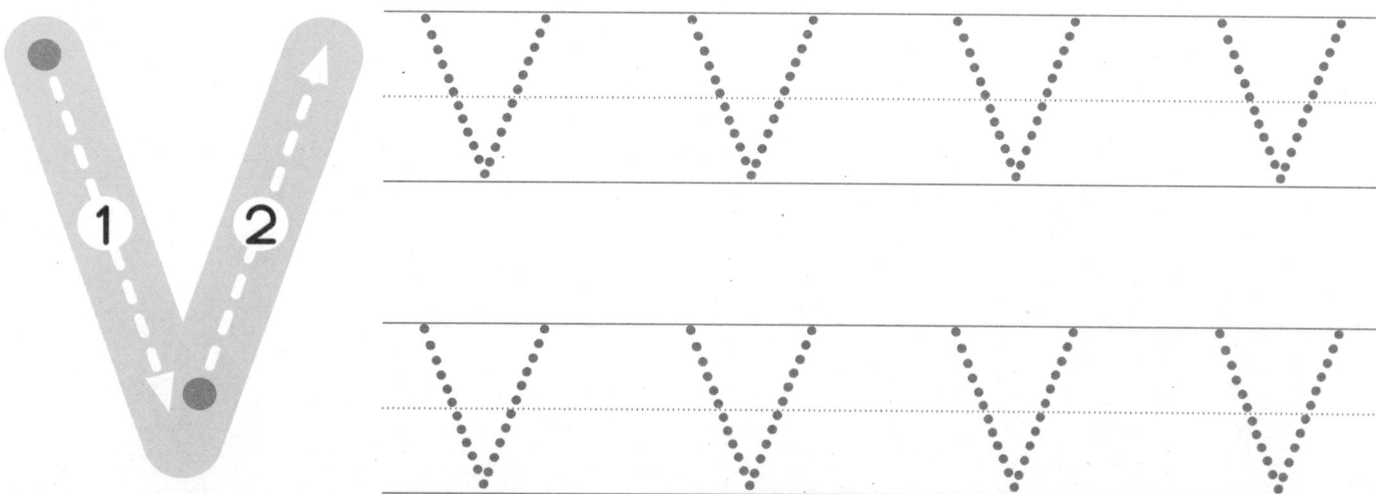

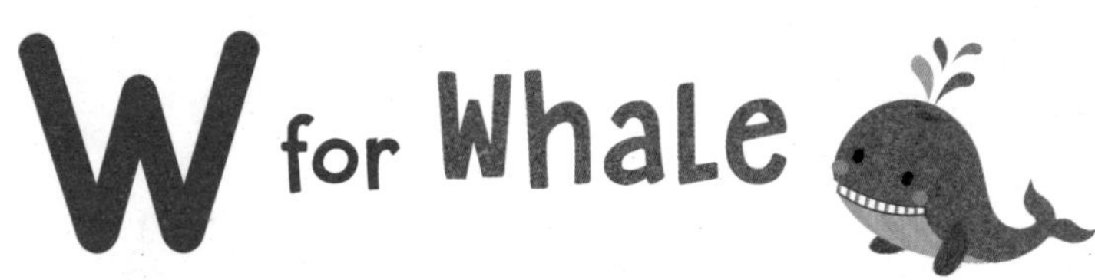

Color the letter W and the WHALE brightly.

Whale

Trace the letter.

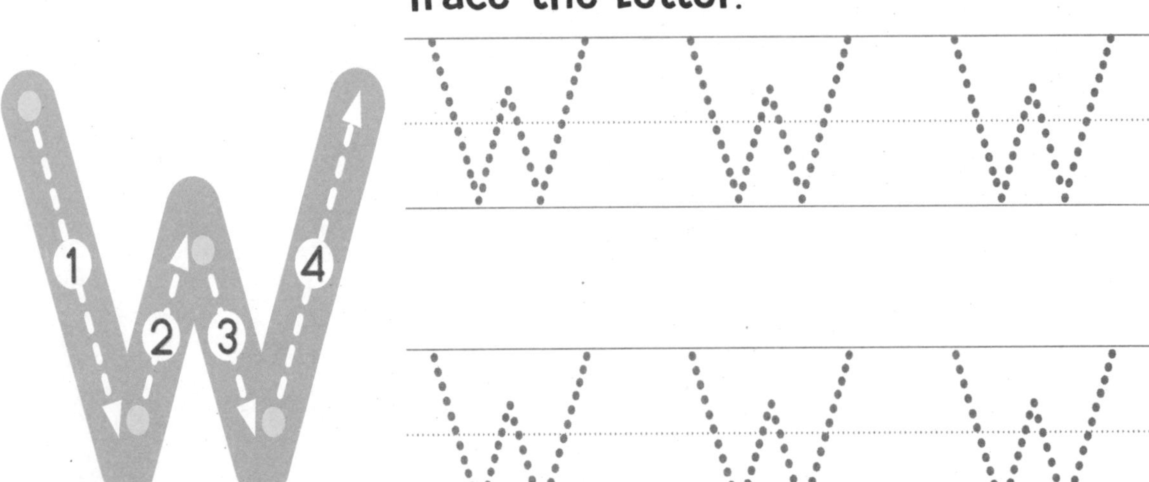

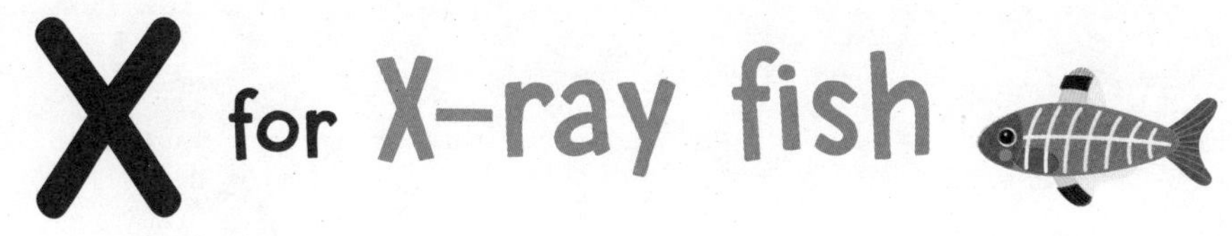
X for X-ray fish

Color the letter X and the X-RAY FISH brightly.

X

X-ray fish

Trace the letter.

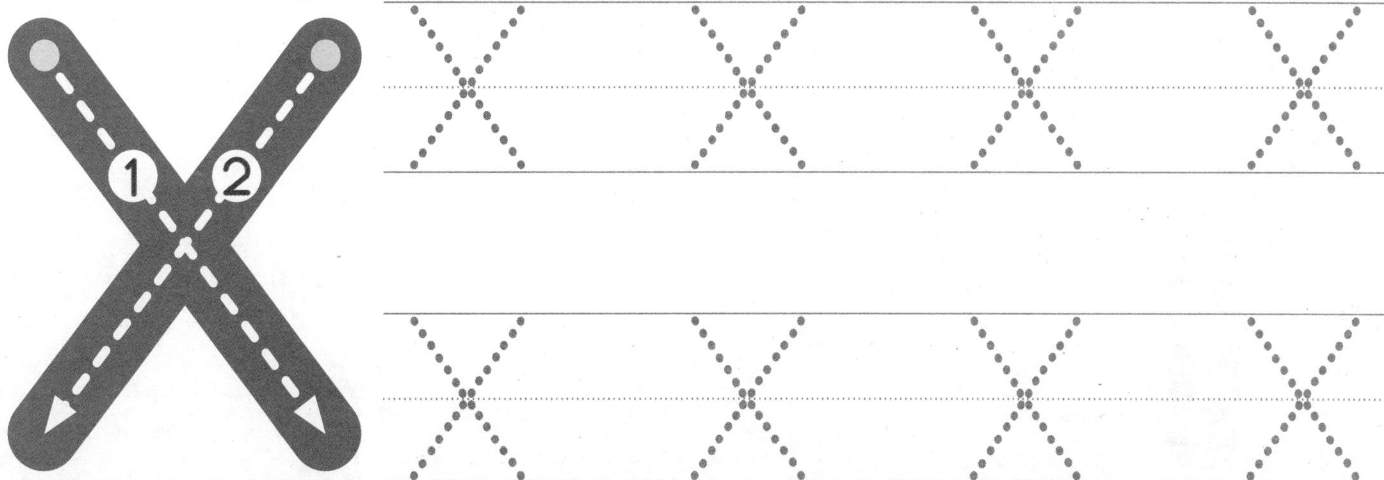

Color the letter Y and the YAK brightly.

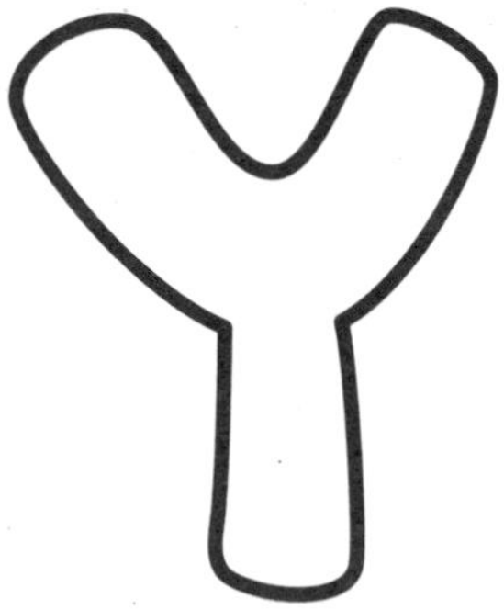

Yak

Trace the letter.

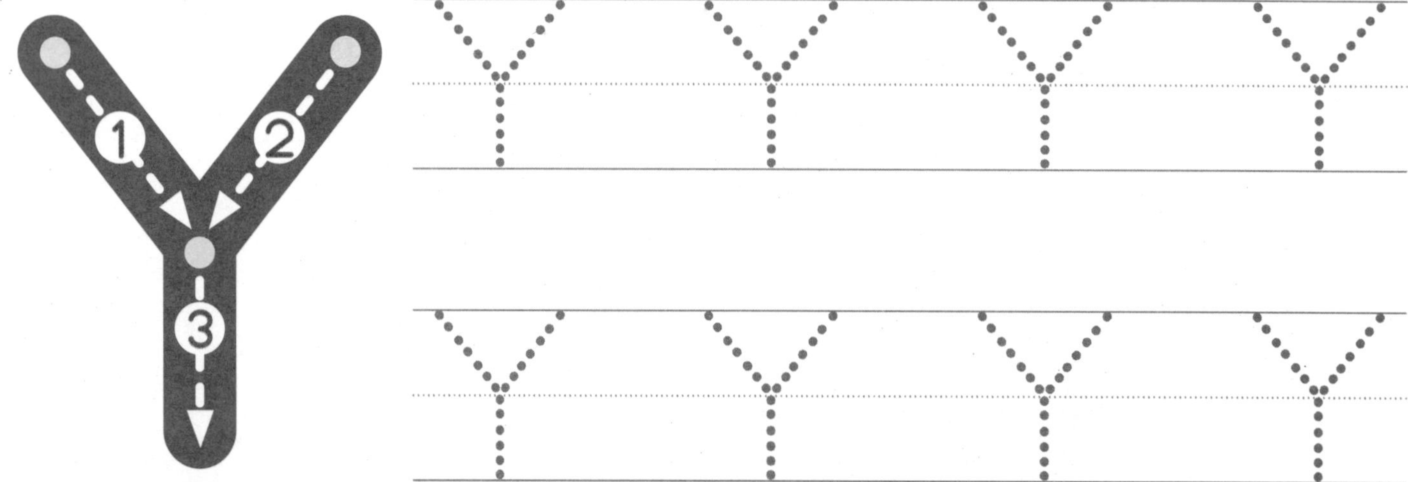

Z for Zebra

Color the letter Z and the ZEBRA brightly.

Zebra

Trace the Letter.

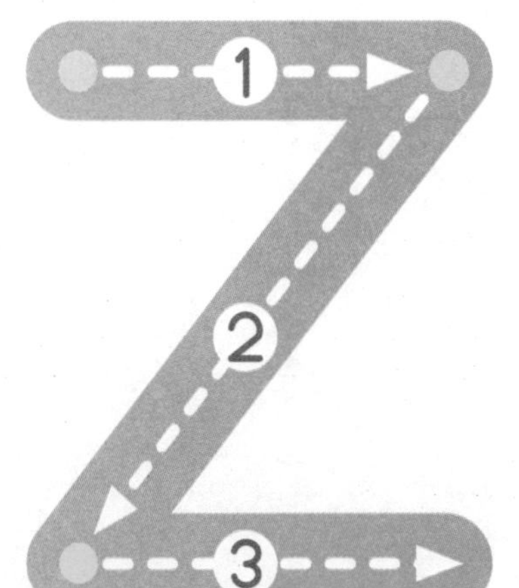

Find the First Letter!

Circle the beginning letter of each picture.

Draw a line from each letter to the picture whose name begins with that letter.

Draw a Circle around the pictures whose name begins with that letter.

Write the missing letters of each word.

_NT

C_NDL_

A__IGATOR

_ARN

_AN

PE_C_L

E_G

_O_KE_

_E_RA

_A_P

_AM

__ANGE

Letter Puzzle

Write the missing letters of each word.

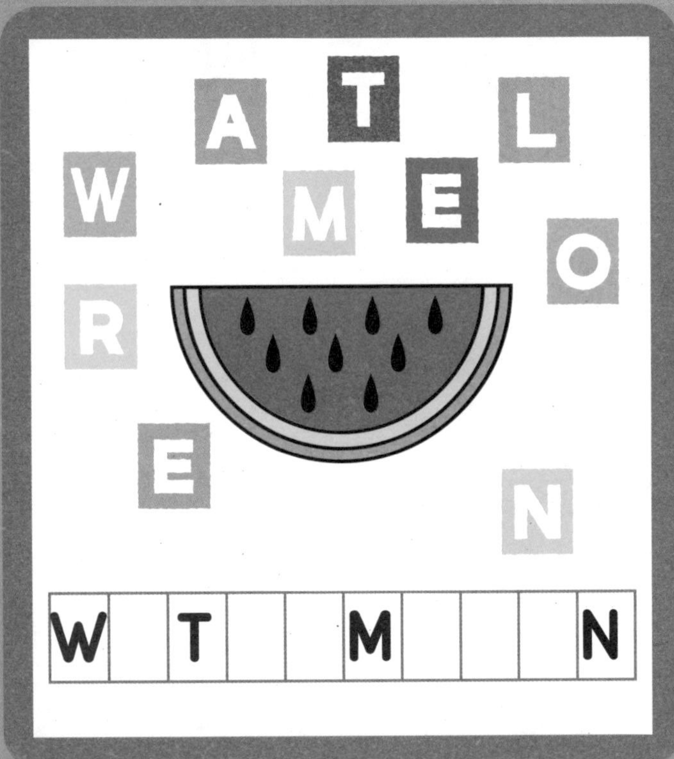

Fill in the Missing Letters.

TRACE

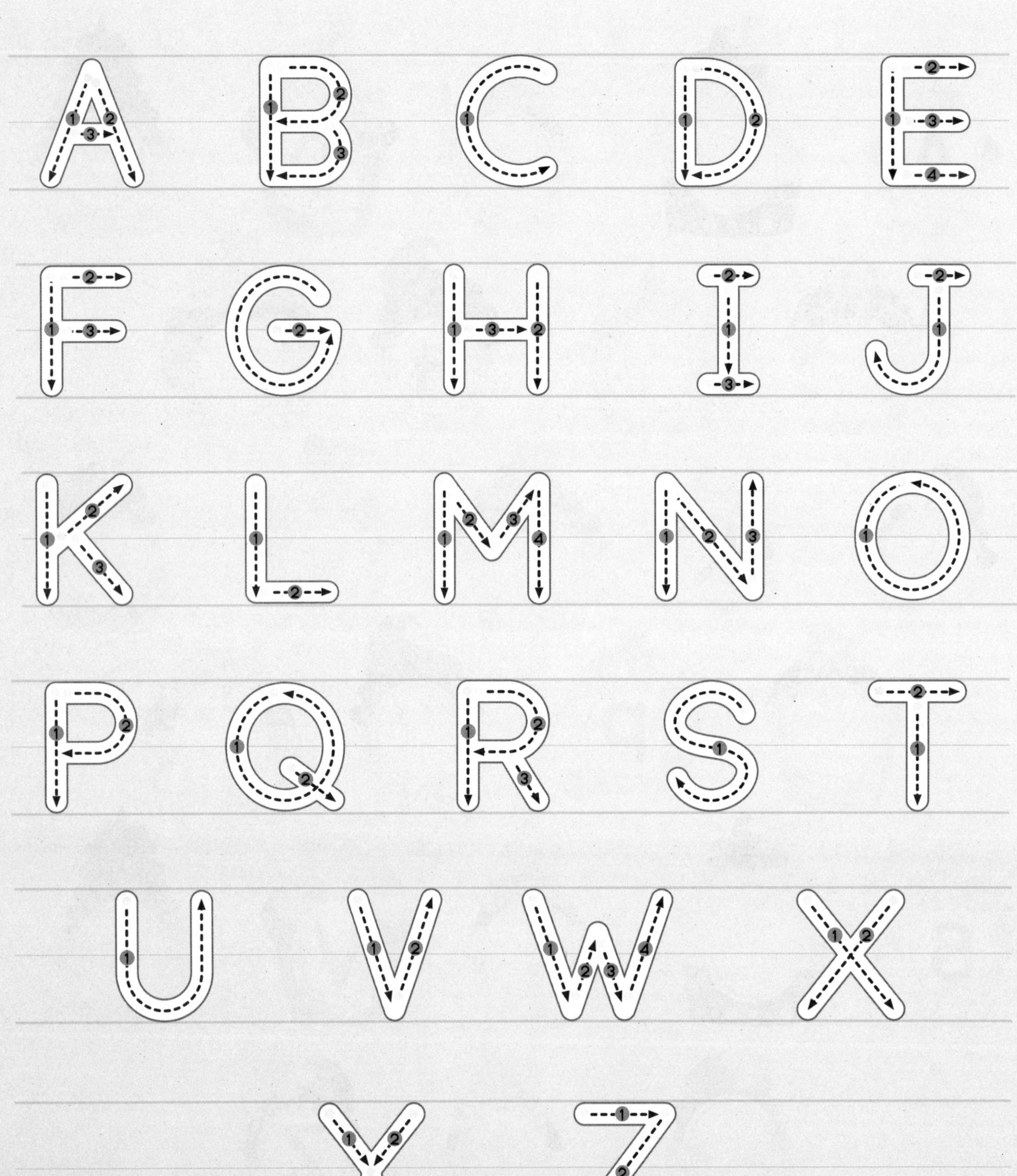

A B C D E
F G H I J
K L M N O
P Q R S T
U V W X
Y Z

ANSWERS

Find the First Letter!
Circle the beginning Letter for each picture.

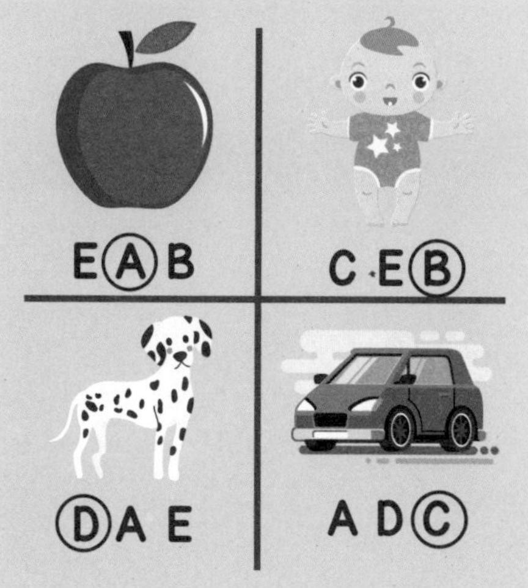

Draw a Circle around the pictures whose name begins with that letter.

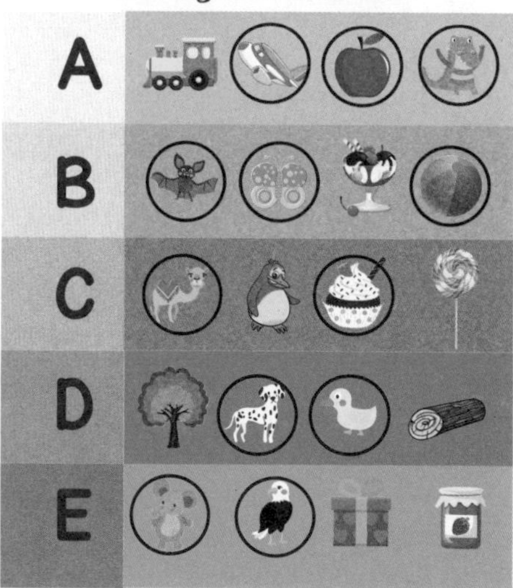

Draw a line from each letter to the picture whose name begins with that letter.

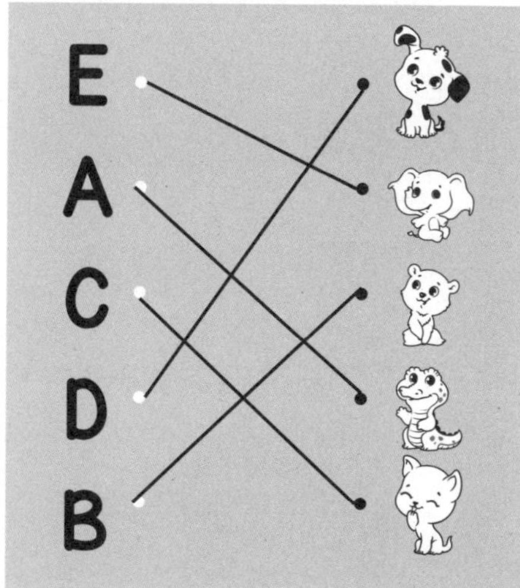

Find the First Letter!
Circle the beginning Letter for each picture.

Draw a Circle around the pictures whose name begins with that letter.

Draw a line from each letter to the picture whose name begins with that letter.

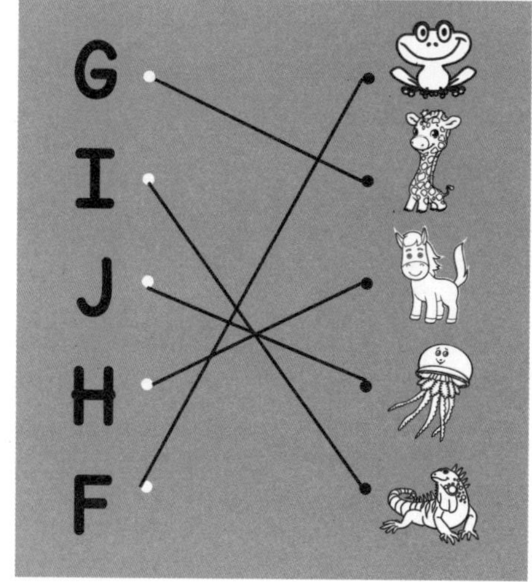

Find the First Letter!
Circle the beginning Letter for each picture.

Draw a Circle around the pictures whose name begins with that letter.

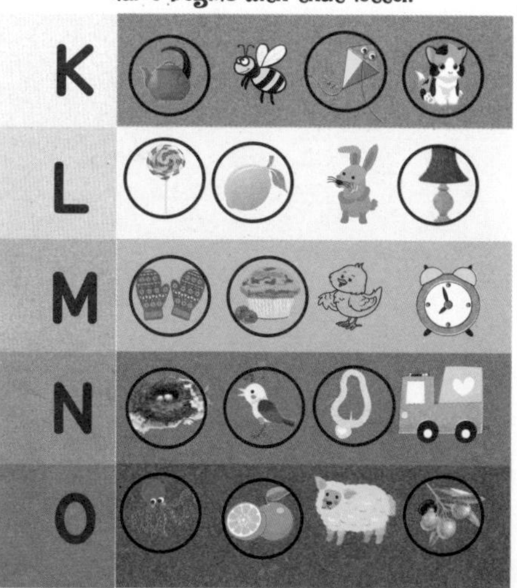

Draw a line from each letter to the picture whose name begins with that letter.

ANSWERS

Find the First Letter!
Circle the beginning Letter for each picture.

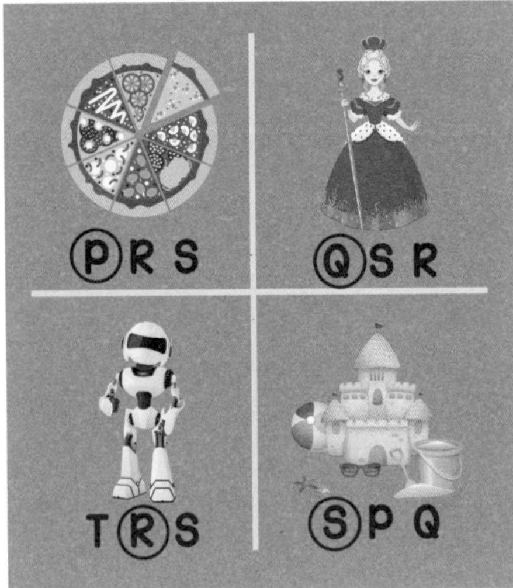

Draw a Circle around the pictures whose name begins with that letter.

Draw a line from each letter to the picture whose name begins with that letter.

Find the First Letter!
Circle the beginning Letter for each picture.

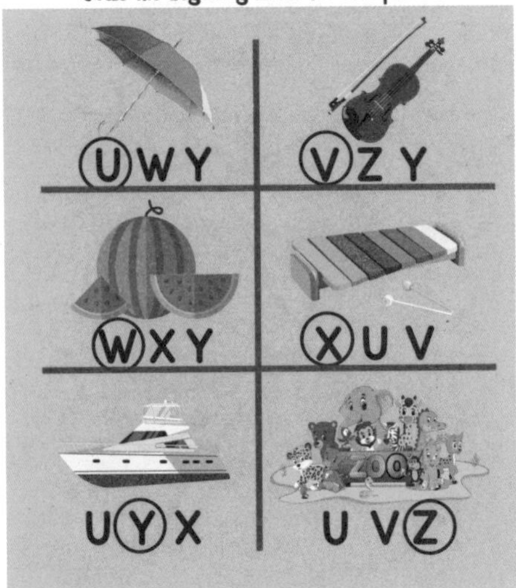

Draw a line from each letter to the picture whose name begins with that letter.

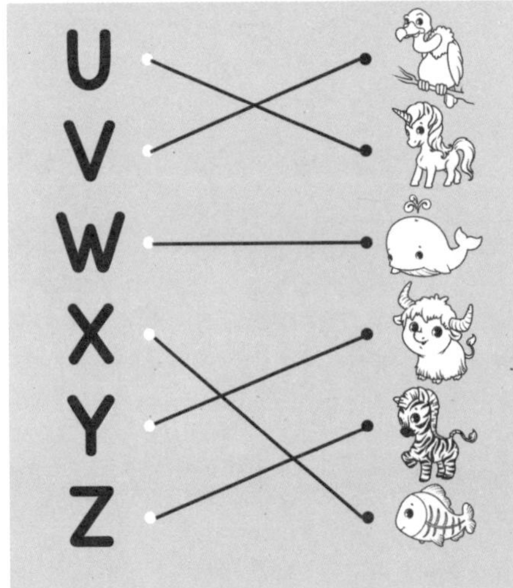

Draw a Circle around the pictures whose name begins with that letter.

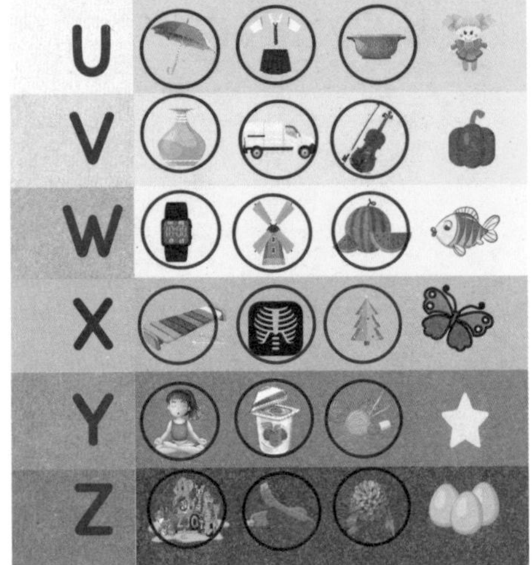

Write the missing letters of each word.

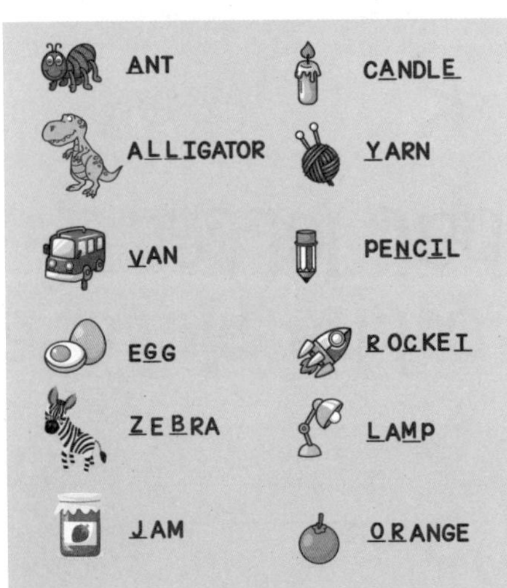

Write the missing letters of each word.

FiLL in the Missing Letters.

My First Book Of Patterns

Small Letters

With Coloring and Activity Pages

a b c

d e f

a for apple

Color the letter a and the apple brightly.

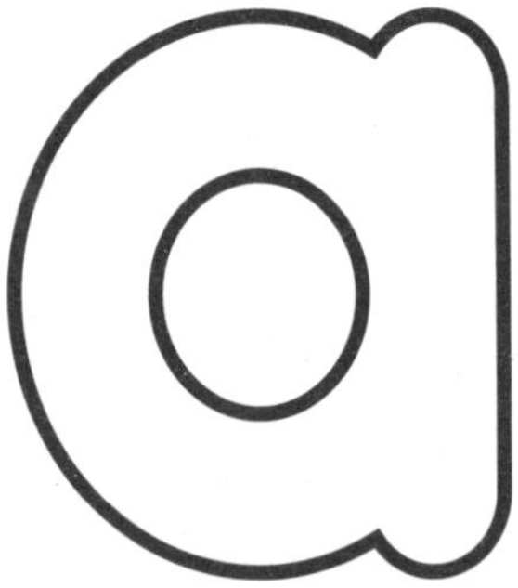

apple

Trace the letter.

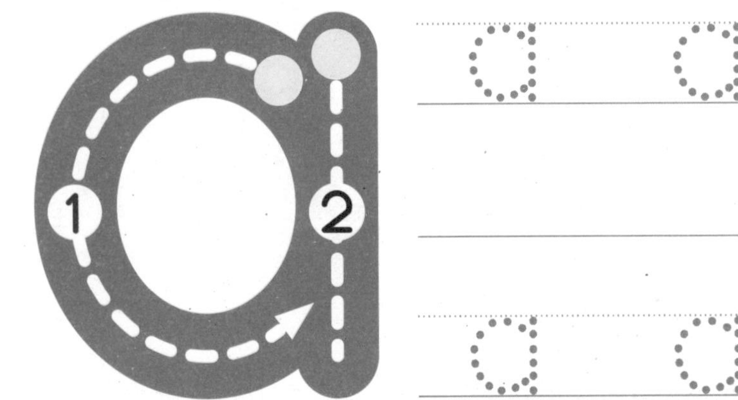

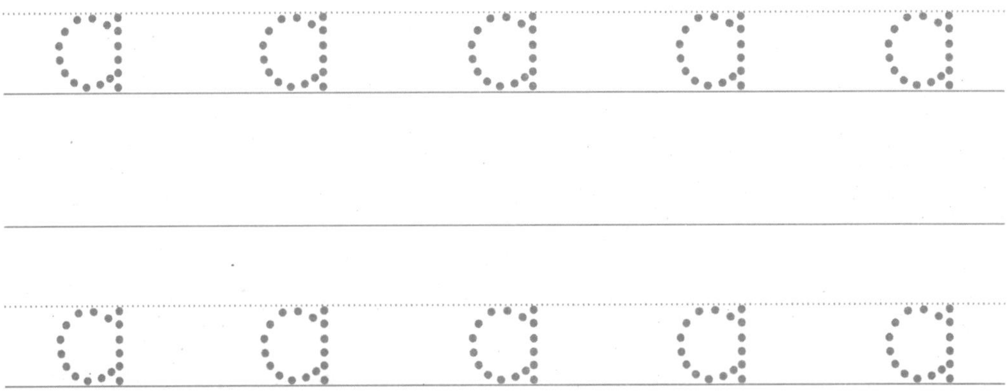

b for ball

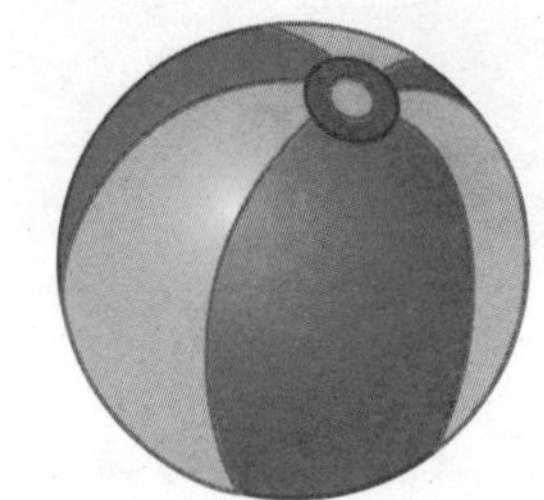

Color the letter b and the ball brightly.

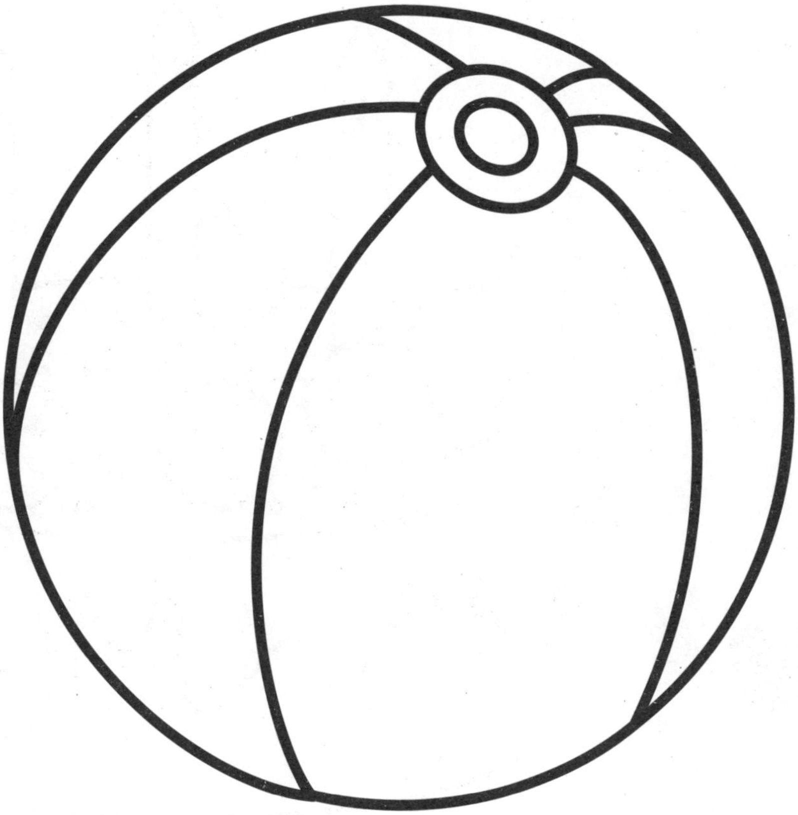

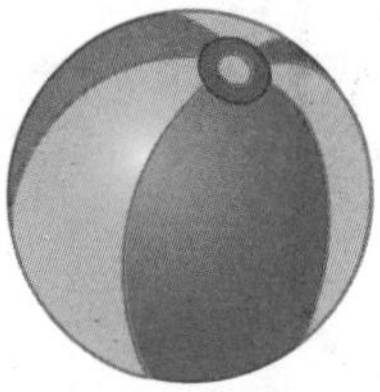

b

ball

Trace the letter.

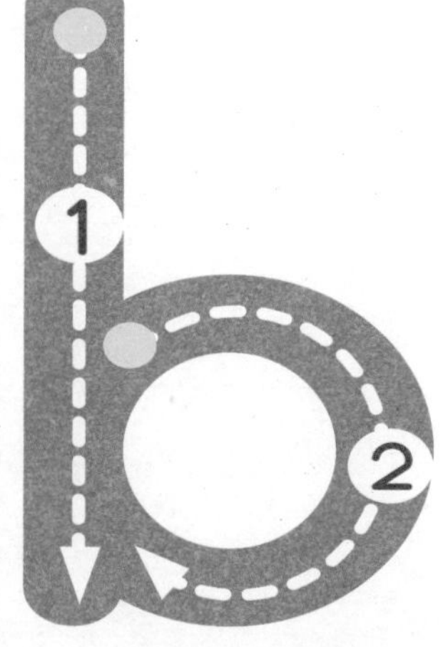

b b b b b

b b b b b

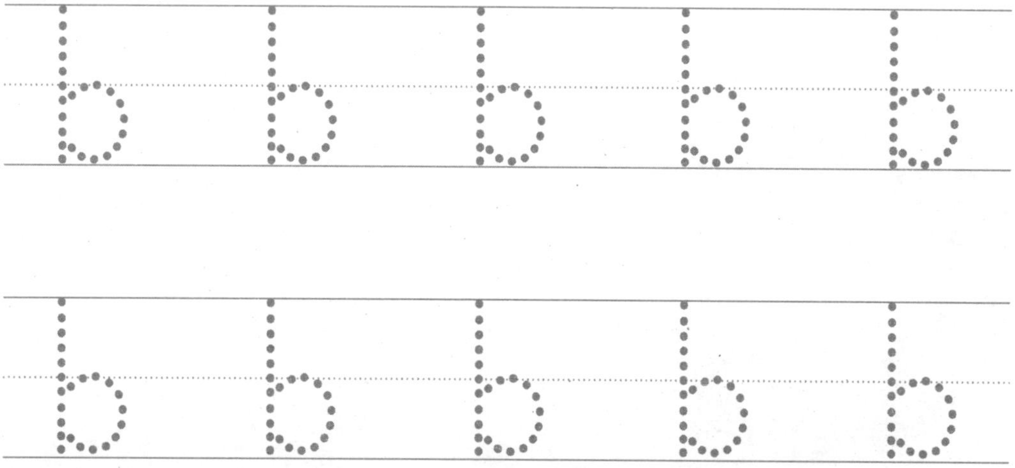

C for cake

Color the letter c and the cake brightly.

cake

Trace the letter.

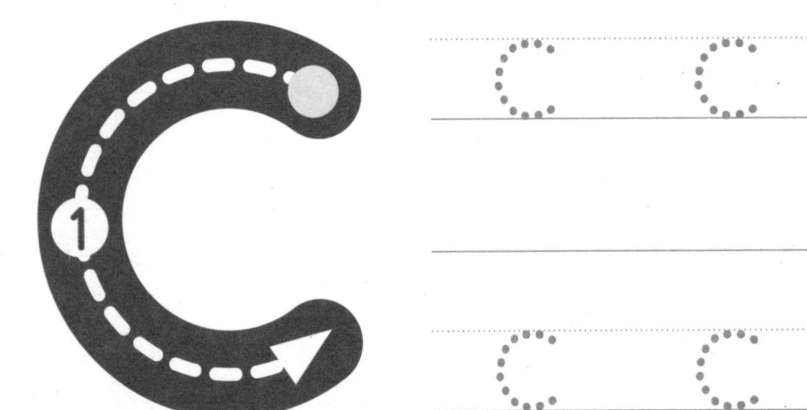

Color the letter d and the doll brightly.

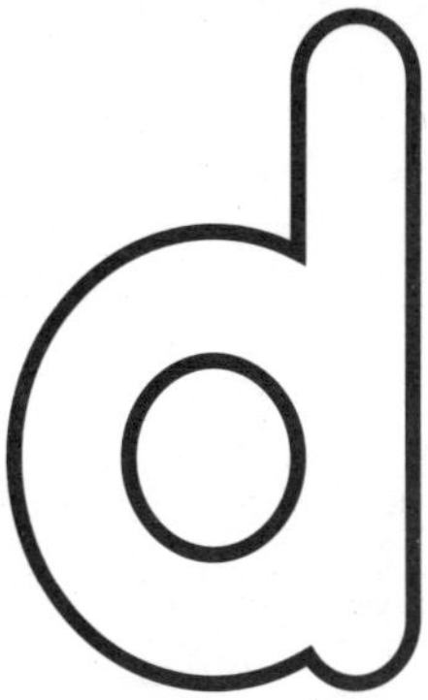

doll

Trace the letter.

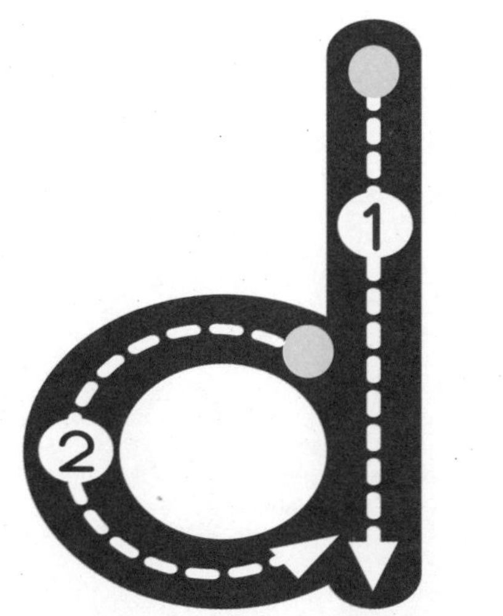

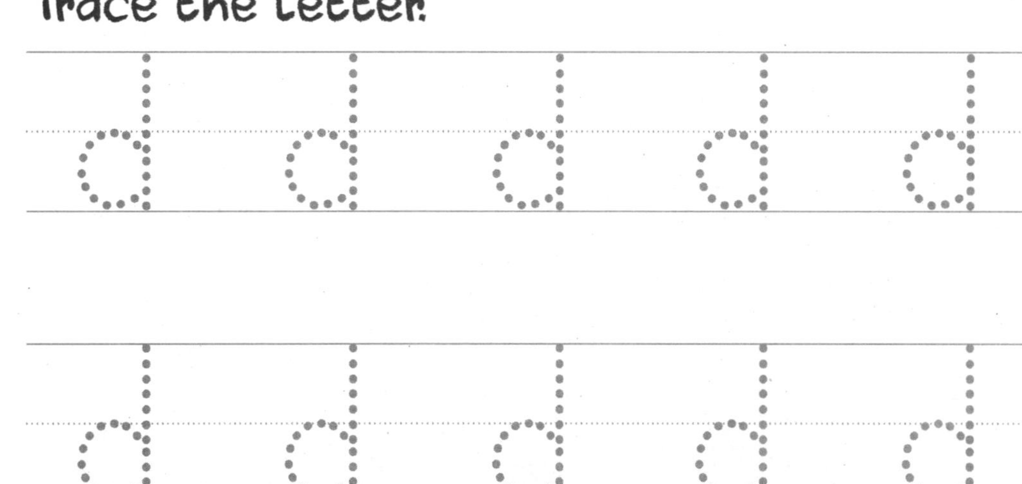

e for egg

Color the letter e and the eggs brightly.

Trace the letter.

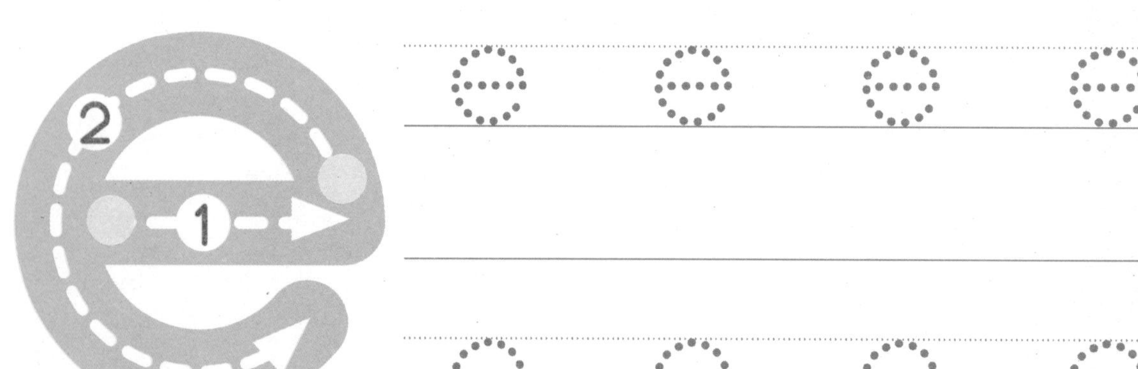

Match Them Up!

Trace the given letters and match with the correct picture.

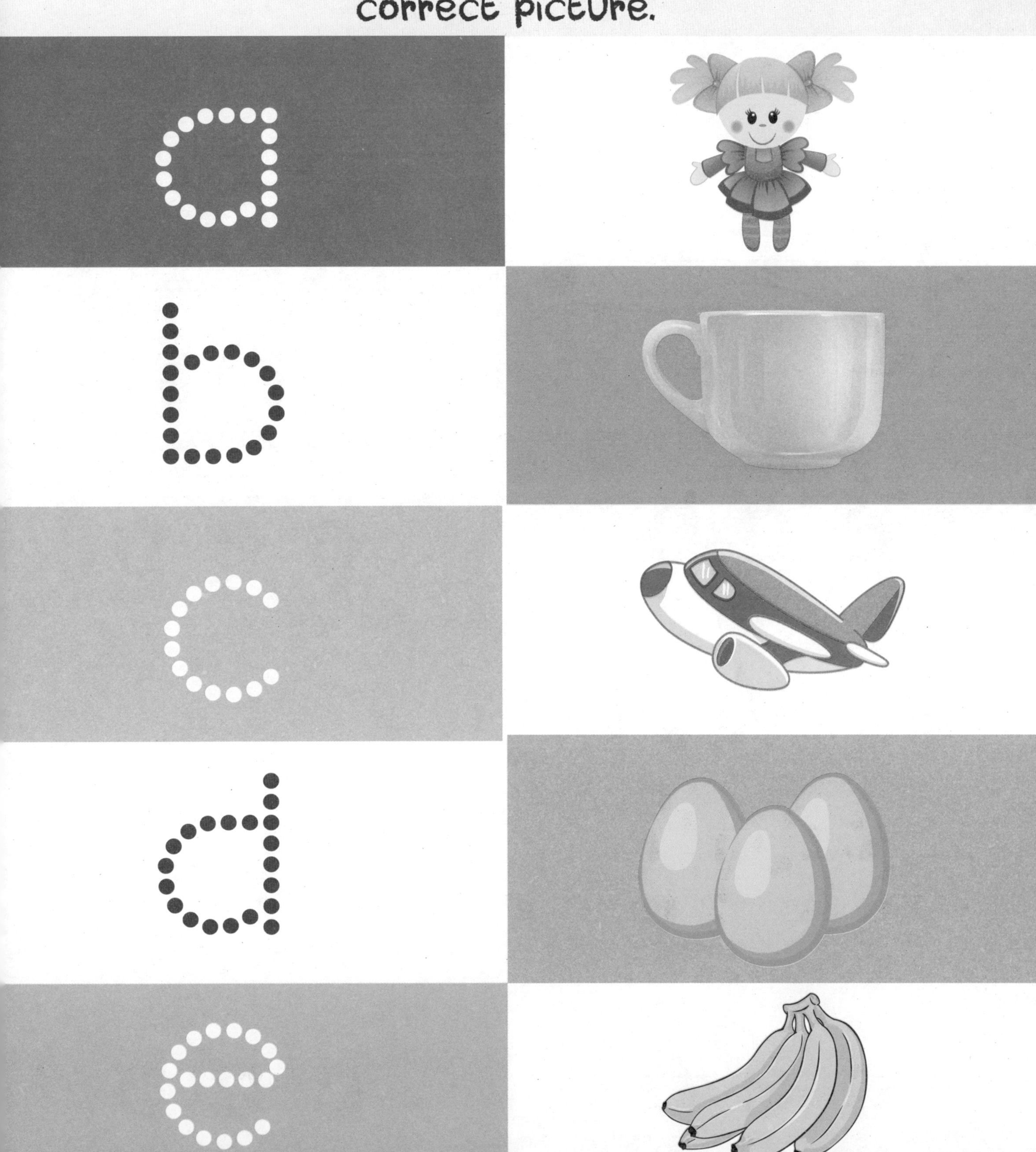

Find the First Letter!

Circle the beginning letter of each picture.

e a b

c e b

d e a

c a b

Circle the Matching Letter!

Trace and match the Lowercase Letter with its Uppercase Letter in each row.

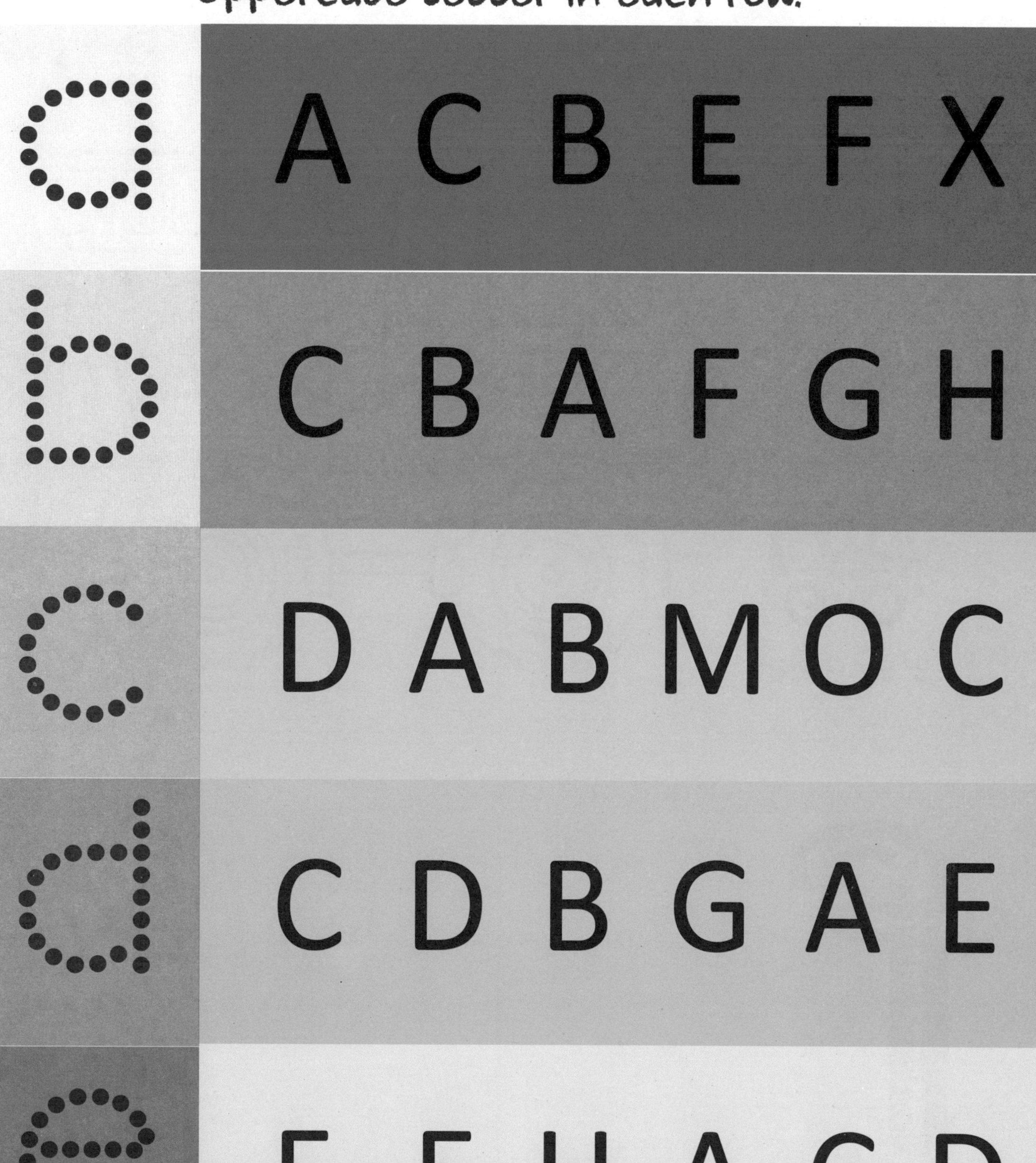

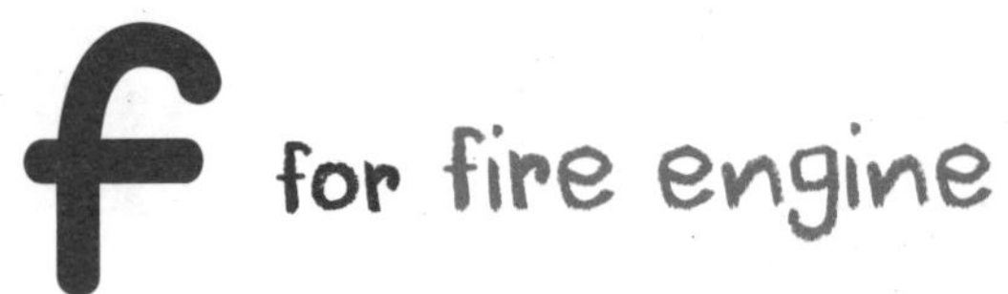
f for fire engine

Color the letter f and the fire engine brightly.

fire engine

Trace the letter.

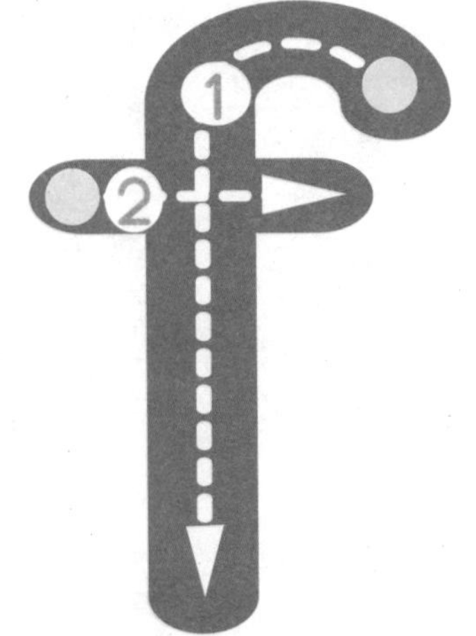

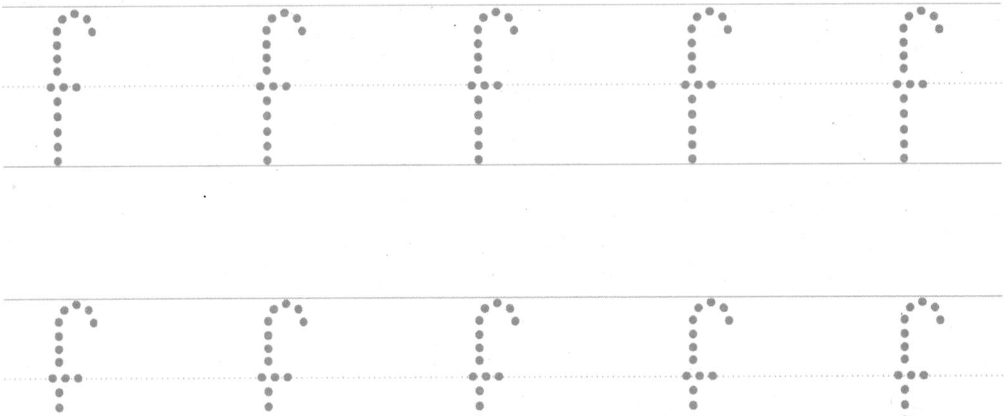

for grape

Color the letter g and the grapes brightly.

grape

Trace the letter.

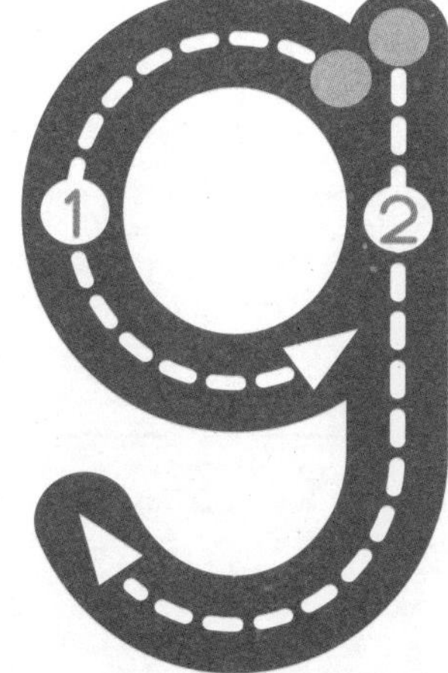

h for hat

Color the letter h and the hat brightly.

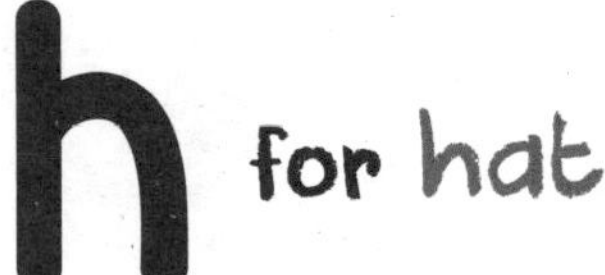

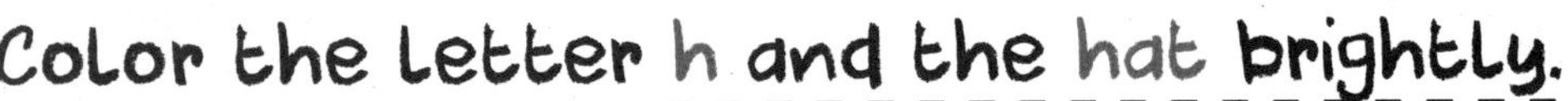

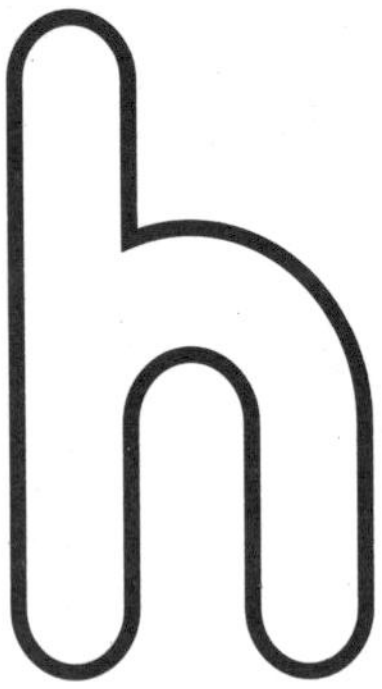

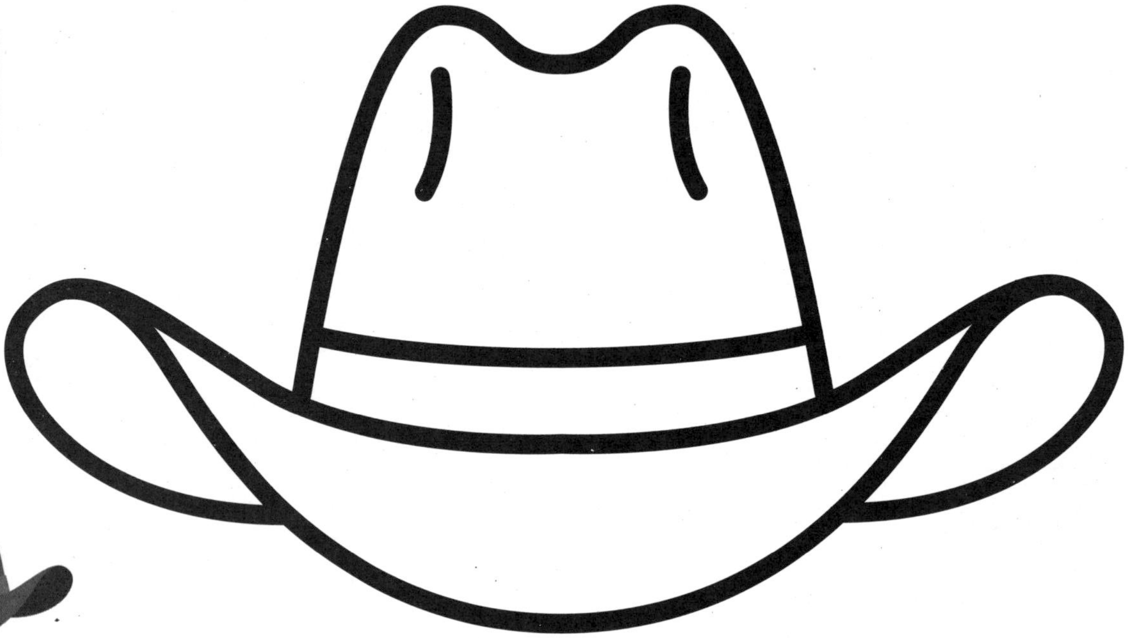

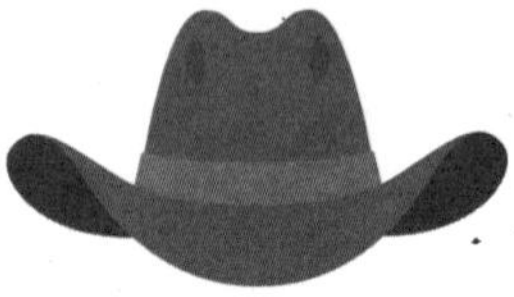

hat

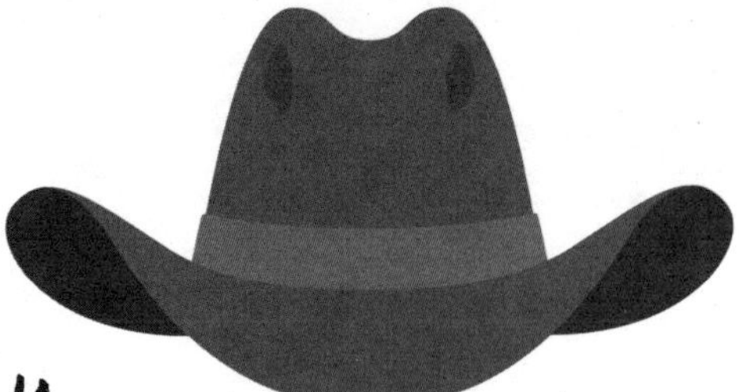

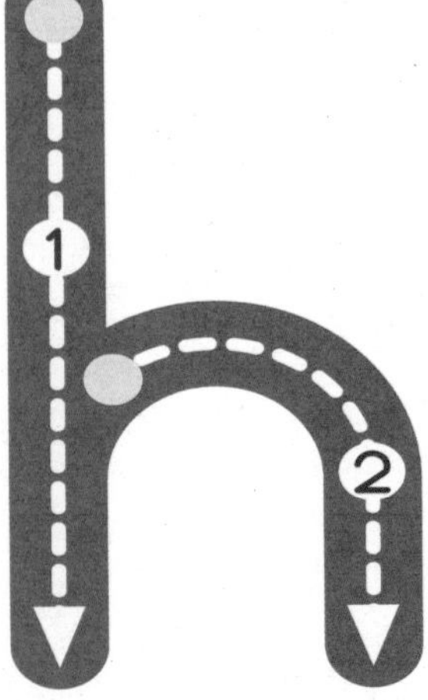

Trace the letter.

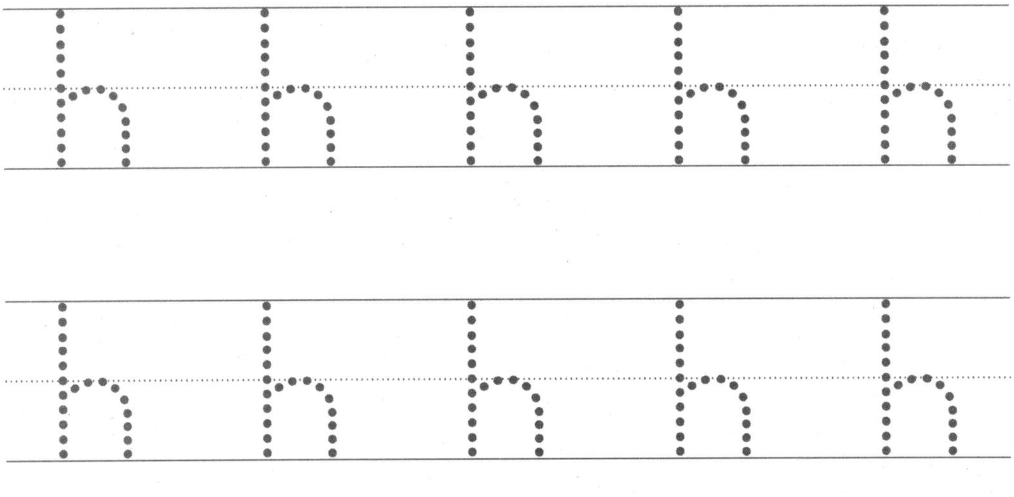

i for ice cream

Color the letter i and the ice cream brightly.

ice cream

Trace the letter.

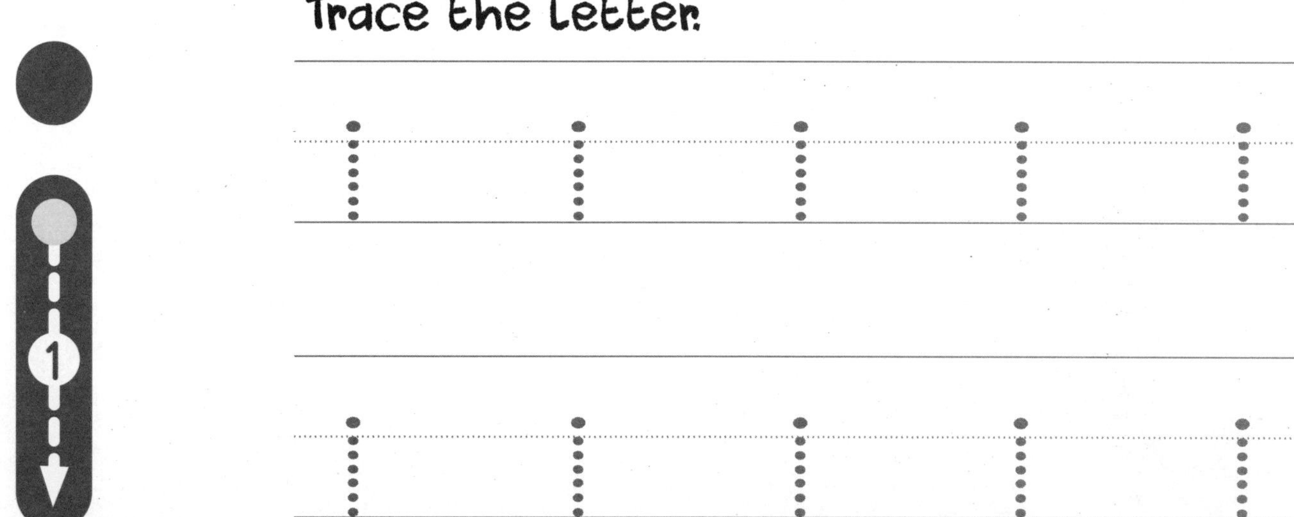

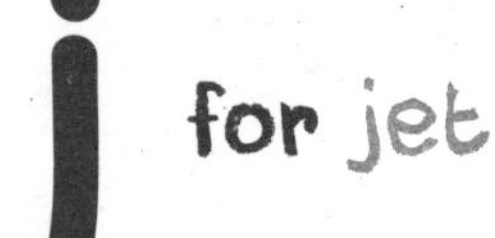 for jet

Color the letter j and the jet brightly.

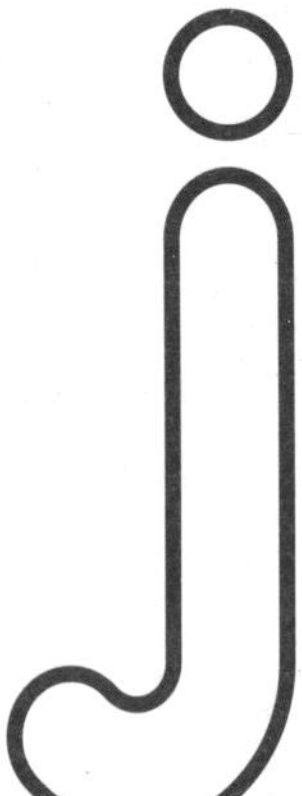

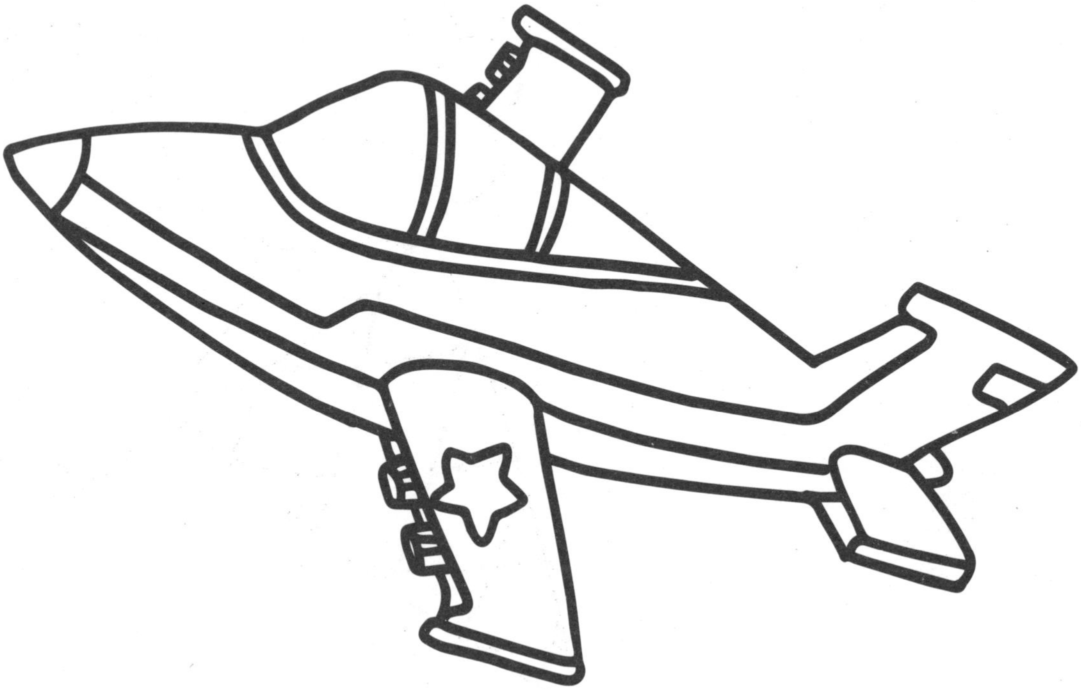

jet

Trace the letter.

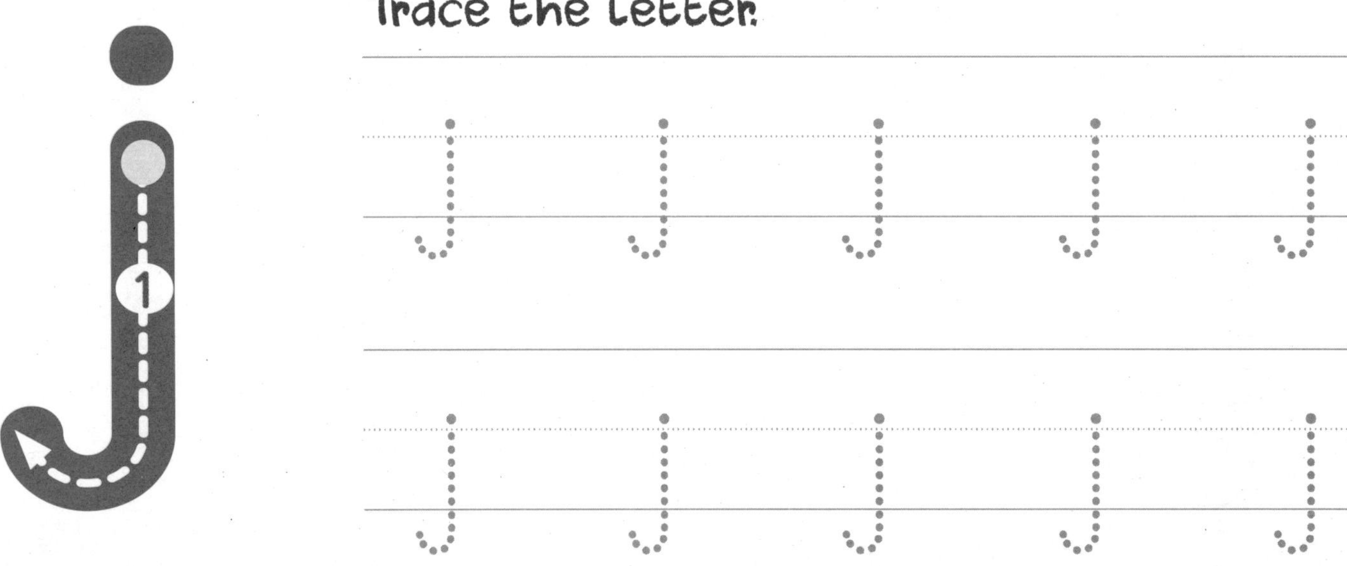

Match Them Up!

Trace the given letters and match with the correct picture.

Find the First Letter!

Circle the beginning letter of each picture.

Circle the Matching Letter!

Trace and match the Lowercase Letter with its Uppercase Letter in each row.

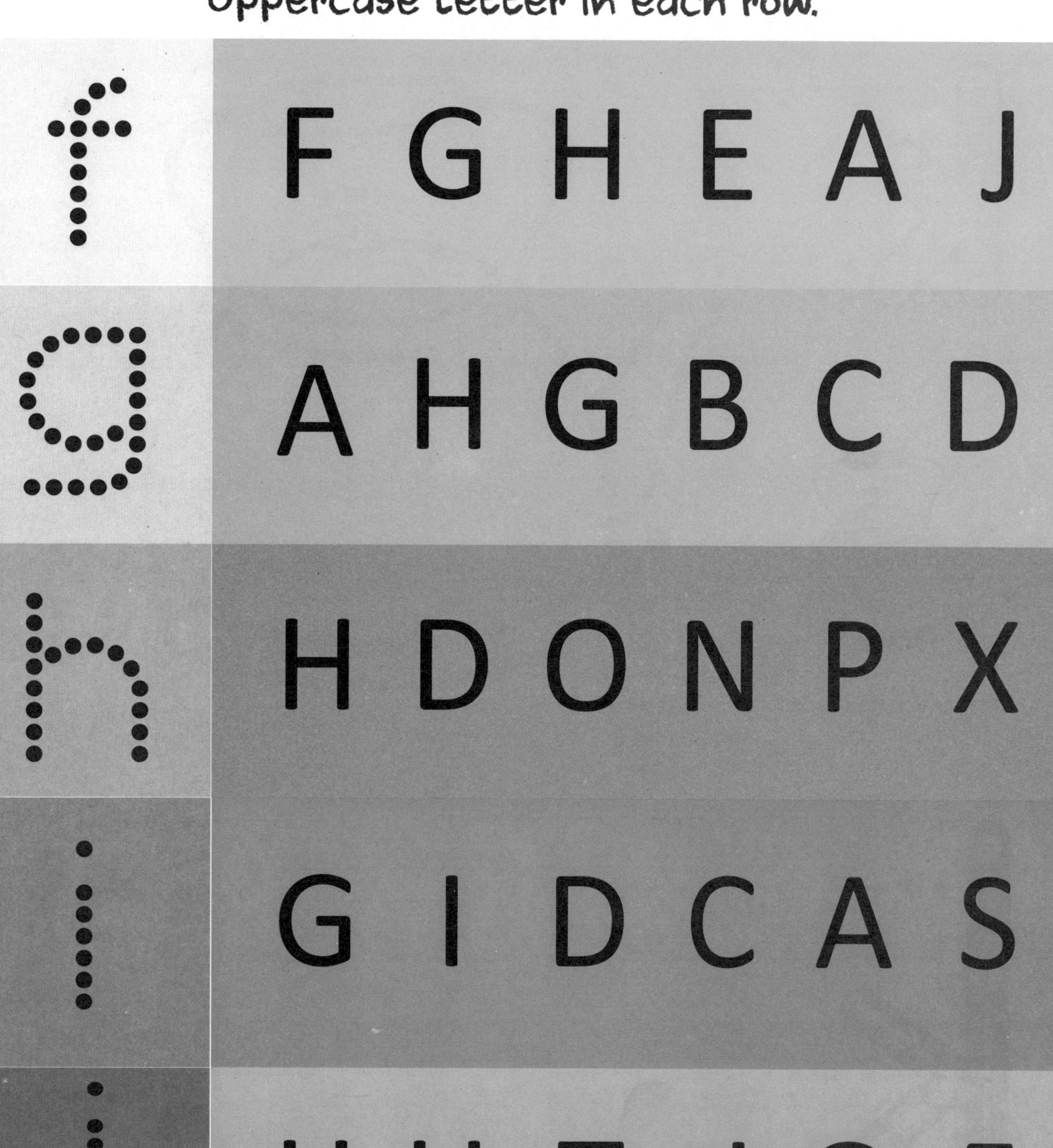

k for kettle

Color the letter k and the kettle brightly.

kettle

Trace the letter.

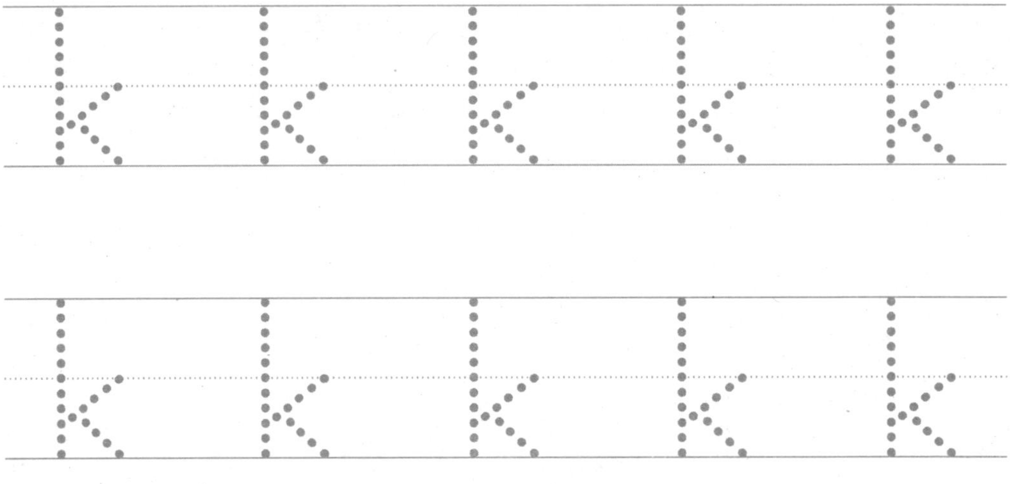

l for lamp

Color the letter l and the lamp brightly.

lamp

Trace the letter.

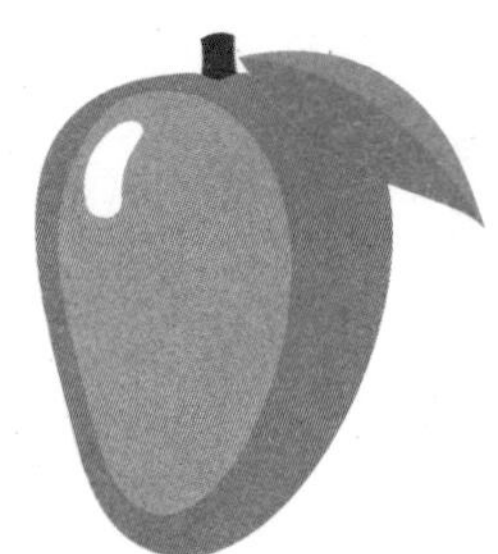

Color the letter m and the mango brightly.

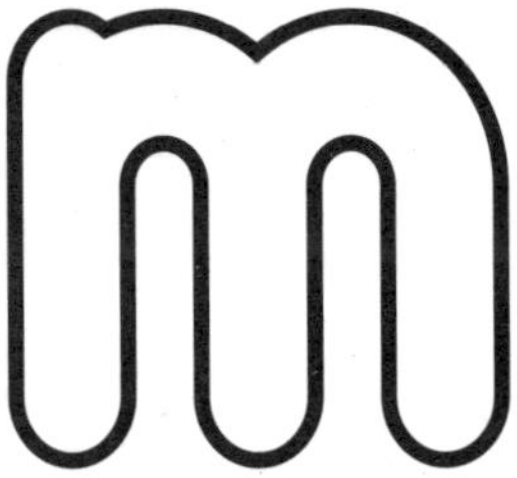

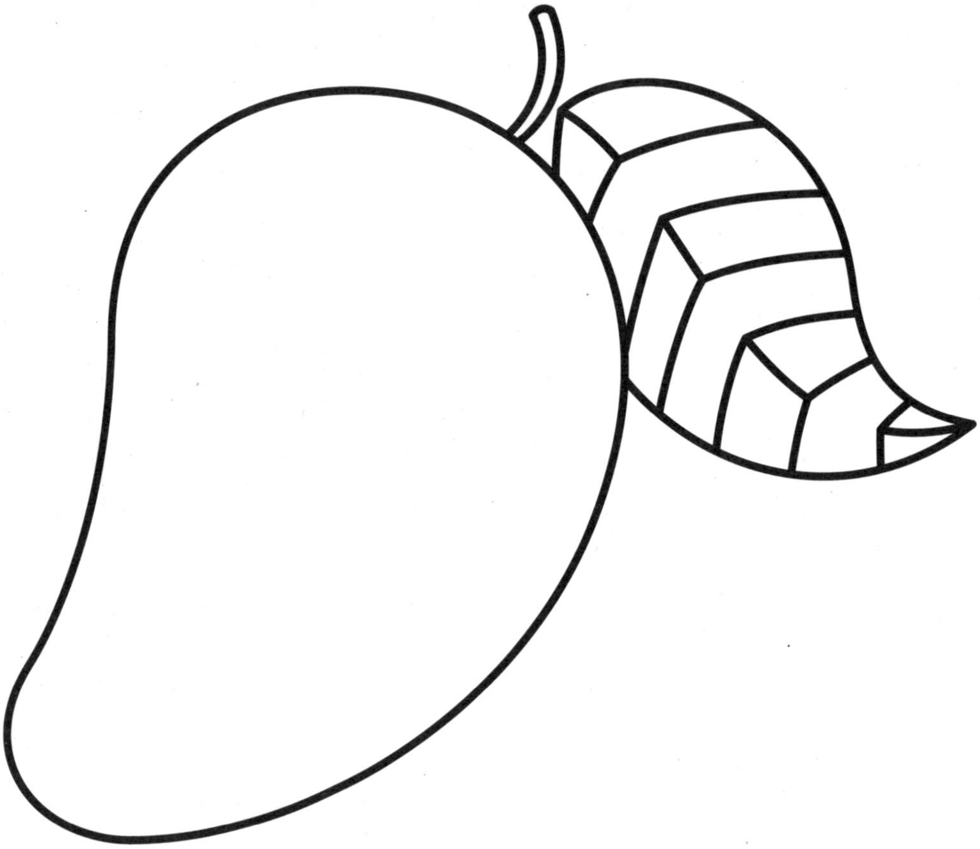

mango

Trace the letter.

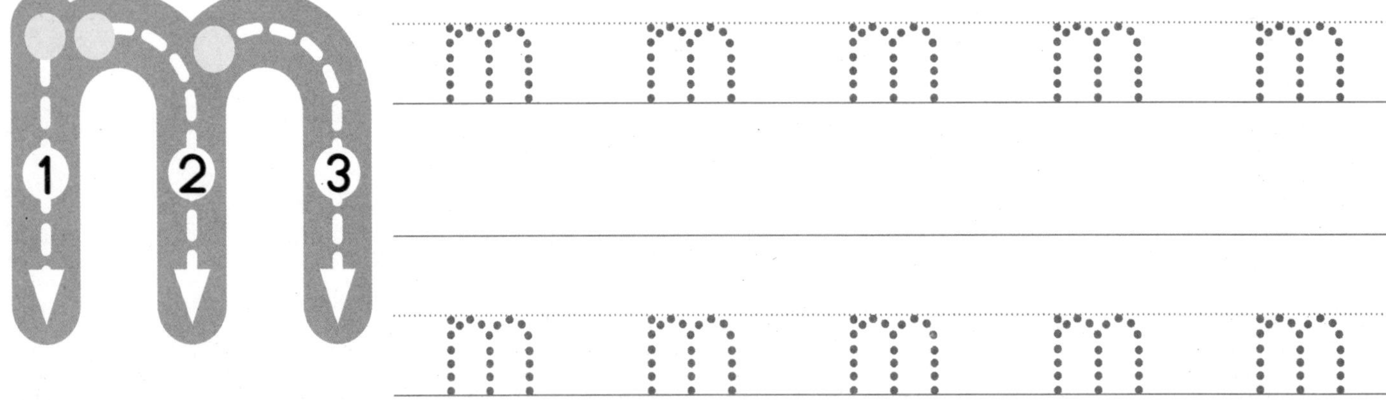

Color the letter n and the necklace brightly.

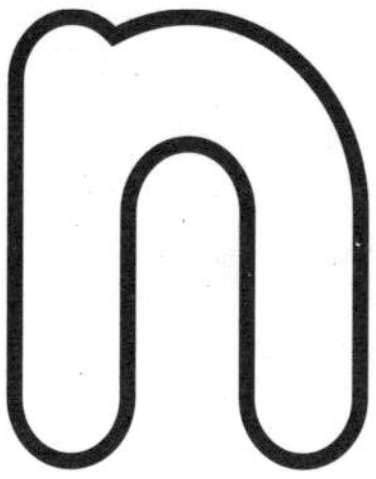

necklace

Trace the letter.

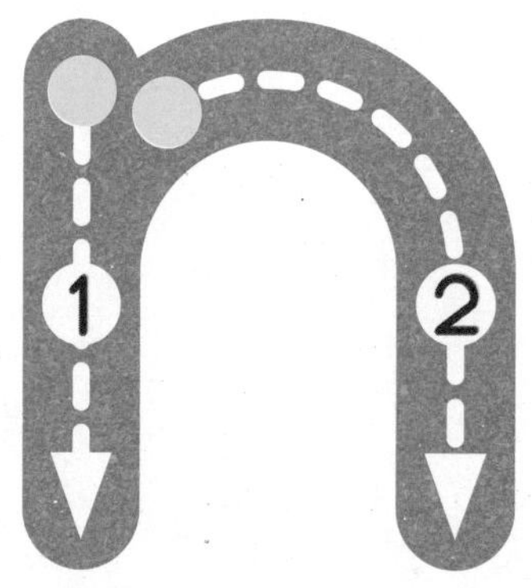

Color the letter o and the orange brightly.

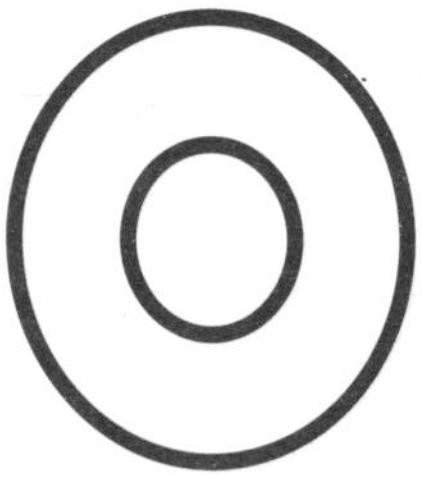

orange

Trace the letter.

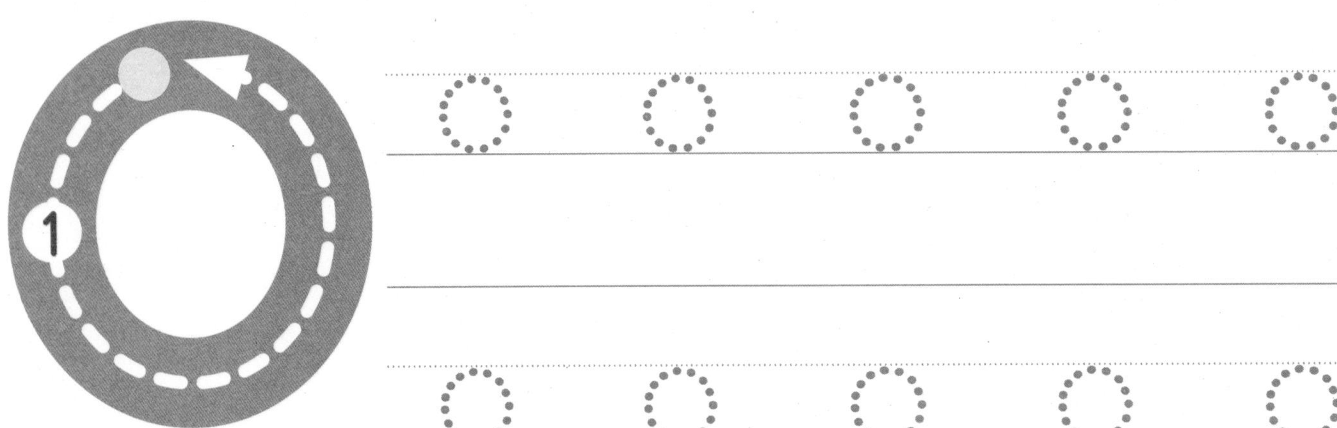

Match Them Up!

Trace the given letters and match with the correct picture.

Find the First Letter!

Circle the beginning letter of each picture.

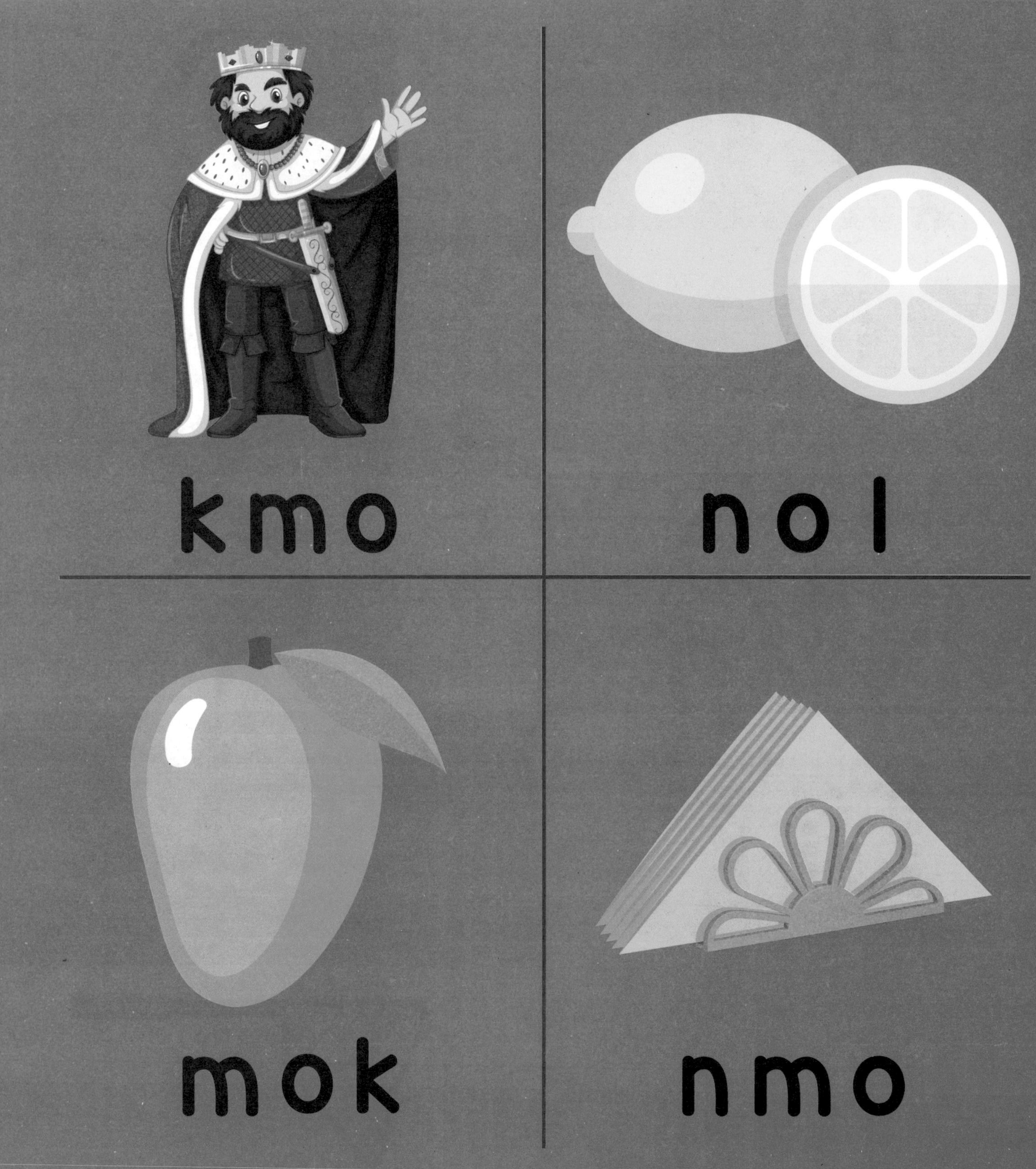

Circle the Matching Letter!

Trace and match the lowercase letter with its Uppercase letter in each row.

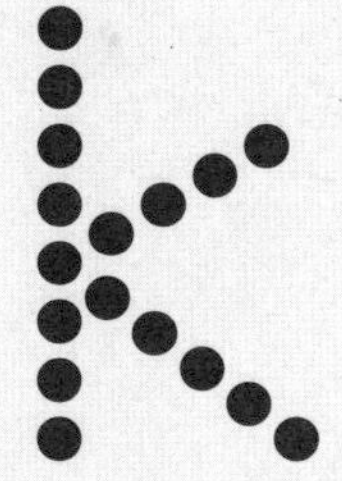	A V K X V G
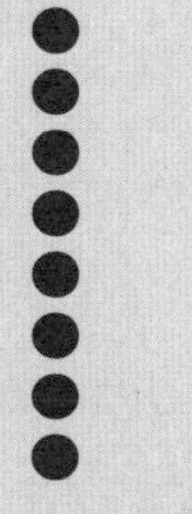	L O H J C A
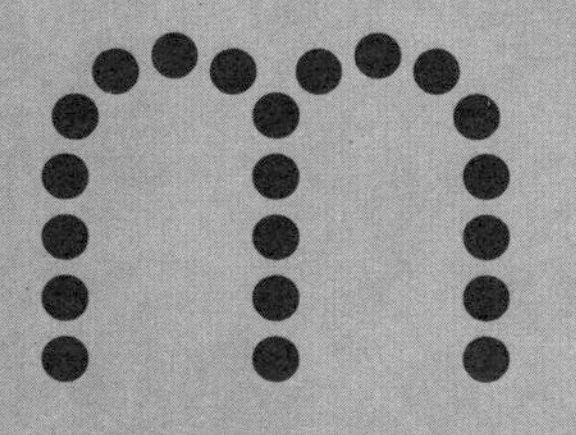	N M O J W R
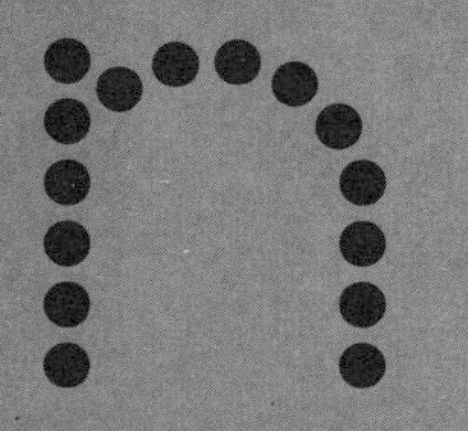	M B N Z A S
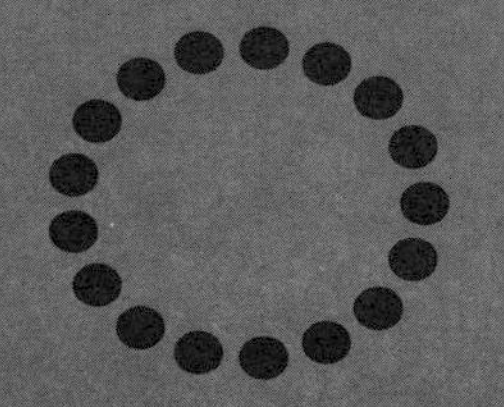	D O P Q G S

for pizza

Color the letter p and the pizza brightly.

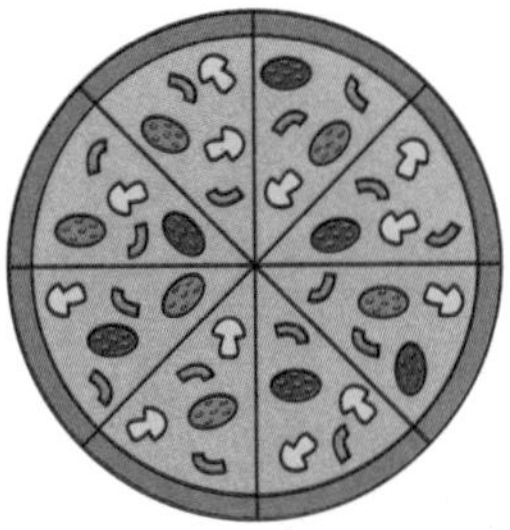

pizza

Trace the letter.

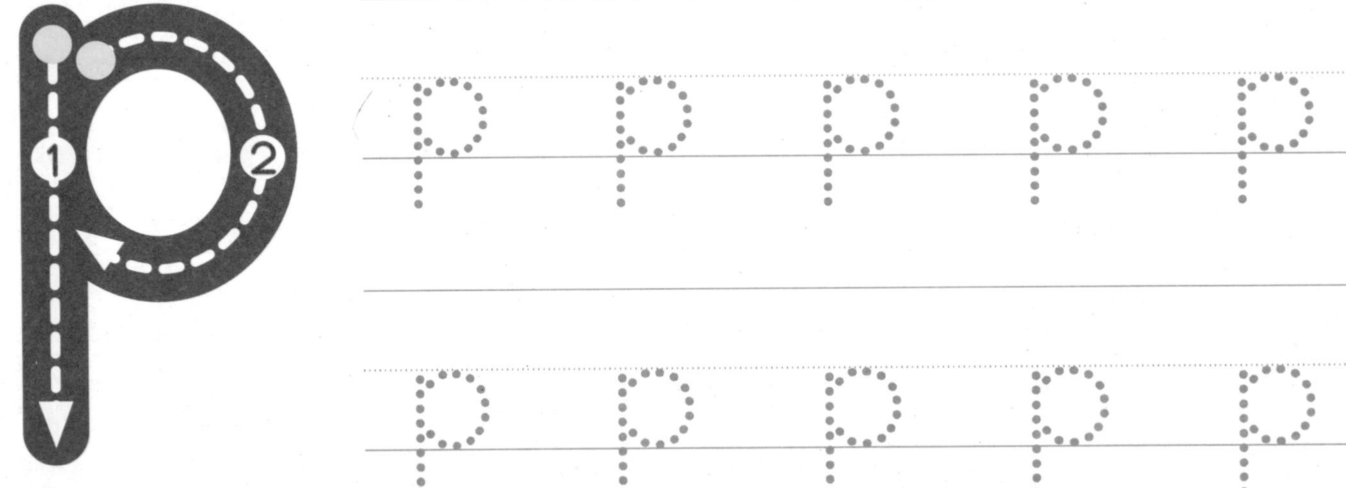

q for queen

Color the letter q and the queen brightly.

Trace the letter.

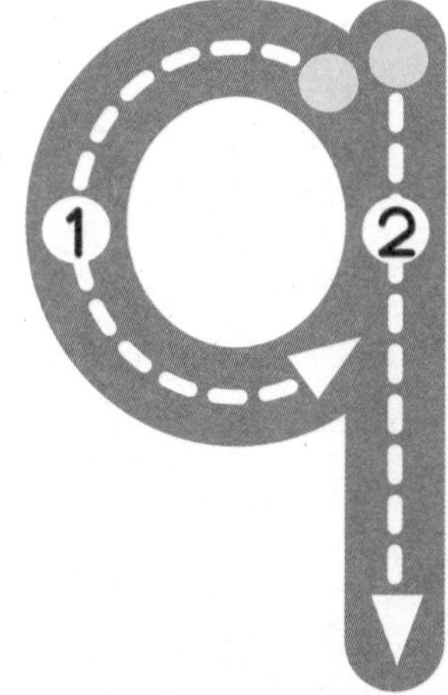

q q q q q

q q q q q

Color the letter r and the rose brightly.

r

rose

Trace the letter.

r r r r r

r r r r r

 for shoes

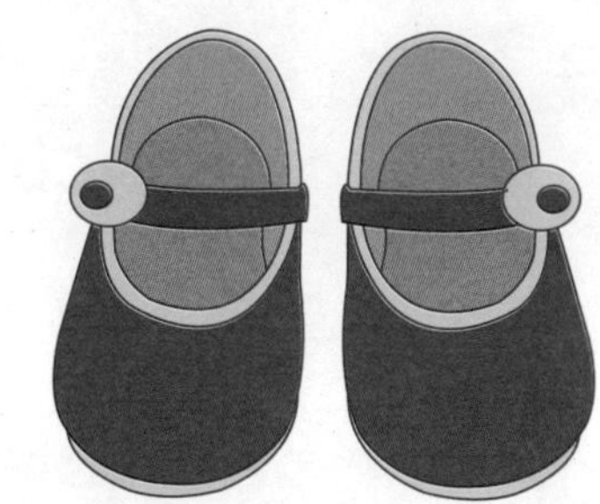

Color the letter s and the shoes brightly.

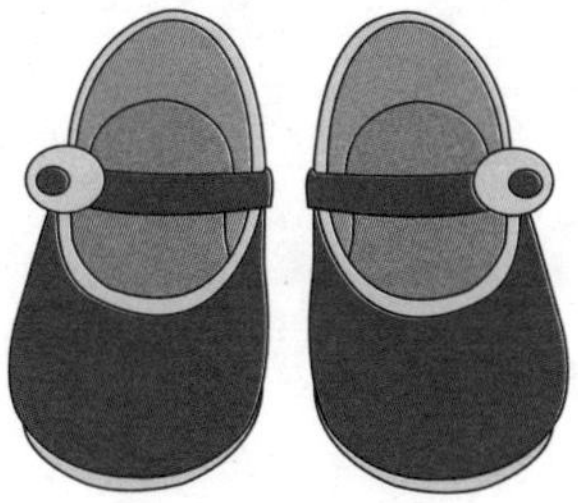

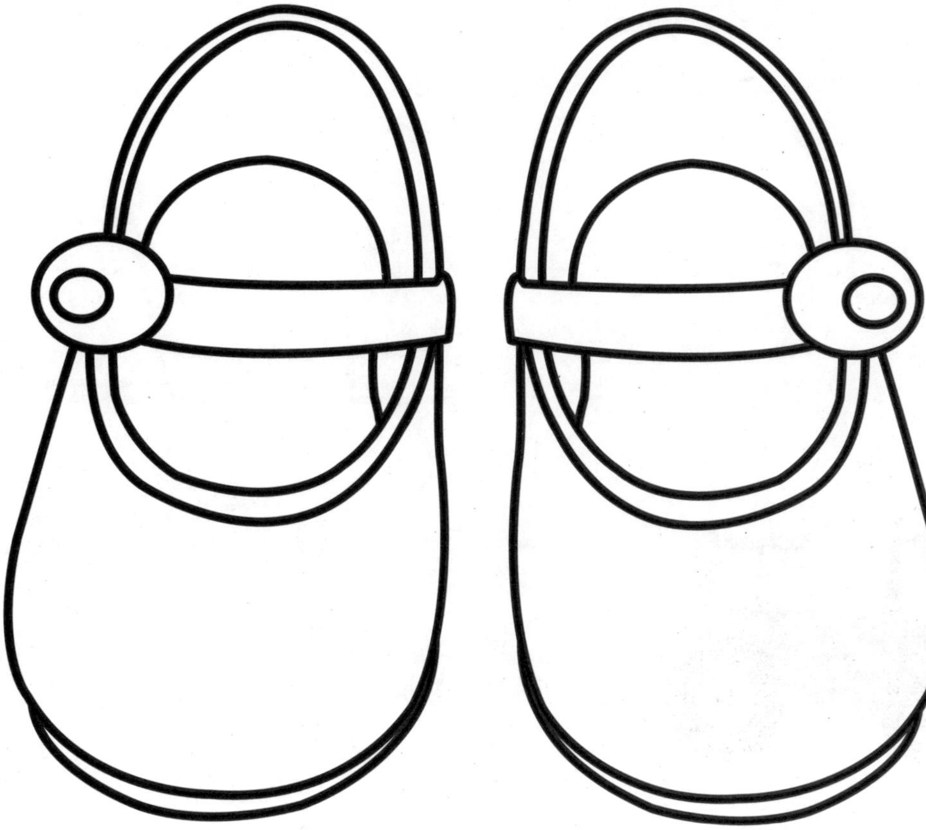

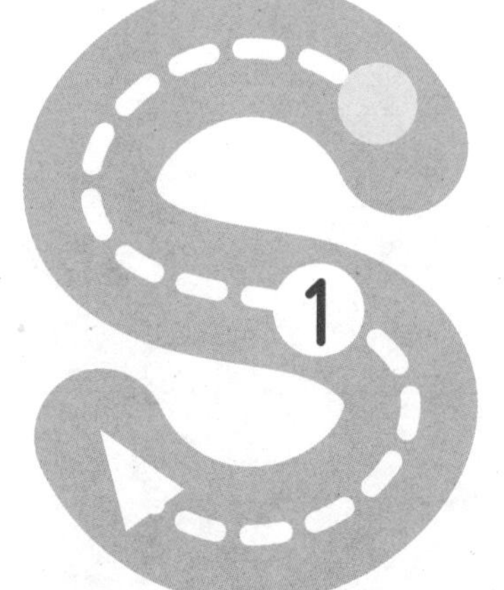

shoes

Trace the letter.

s s s s s

s s s s s

Color the letter t and the tractor brightly.

tractor

Trace the letter.

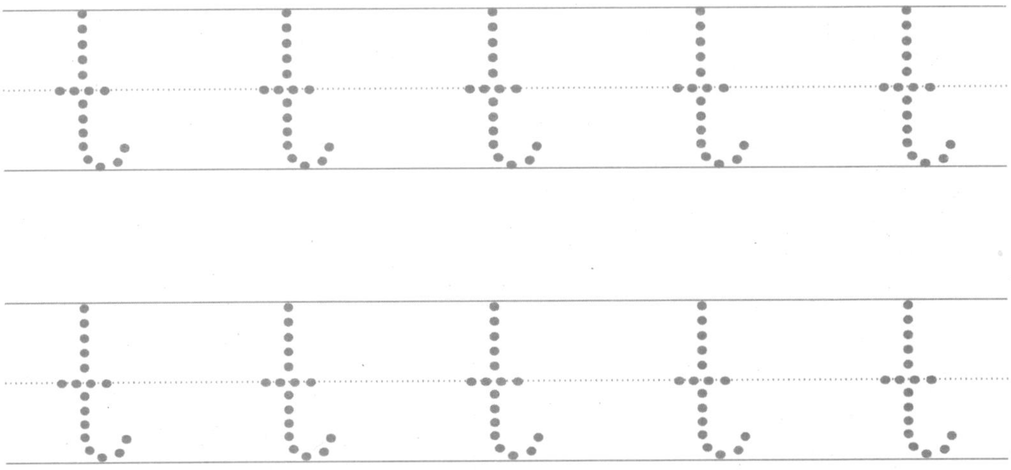

Match Them Up!

Trace the given letters and match with the correct picture.

Find the First Letter!

Circle the beginning letter of each picture.

p r q

q s r

q r s

p t s

Circle the Matching Letter!

Trace and match the Lowercase Letter with its Uppercase Letter in each row.

D C P B R G

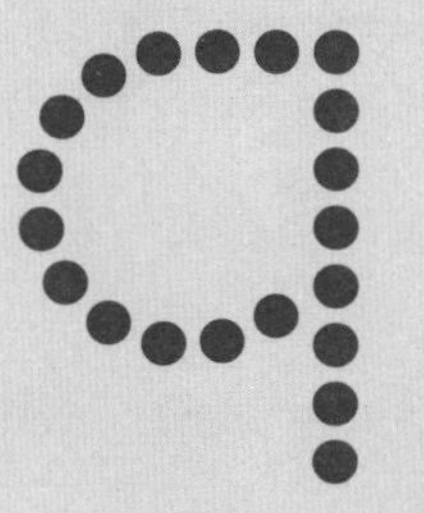

Q O U P D A

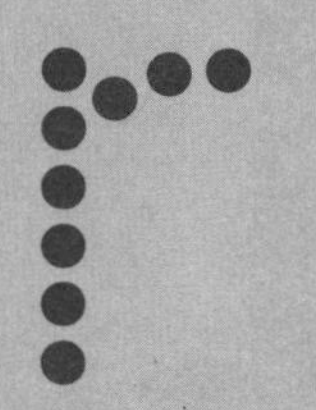

P Q R B D O

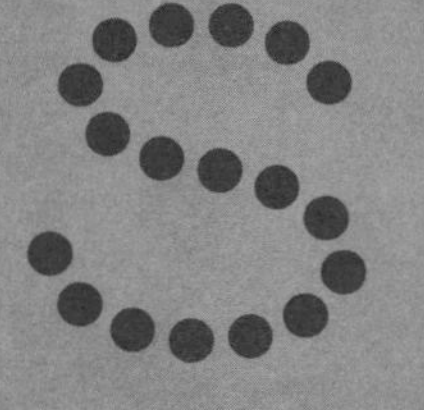

S C E Z B U

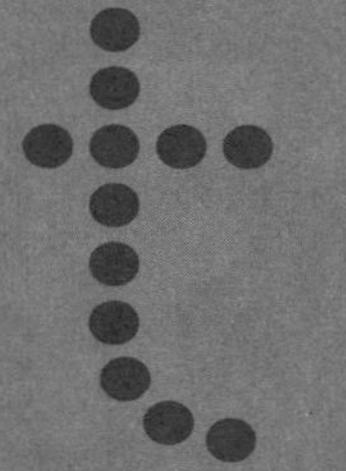

T H F L E B

u for umbrella

Color the letter u and the umbrella brightly.

umbrella

Trace the letter.

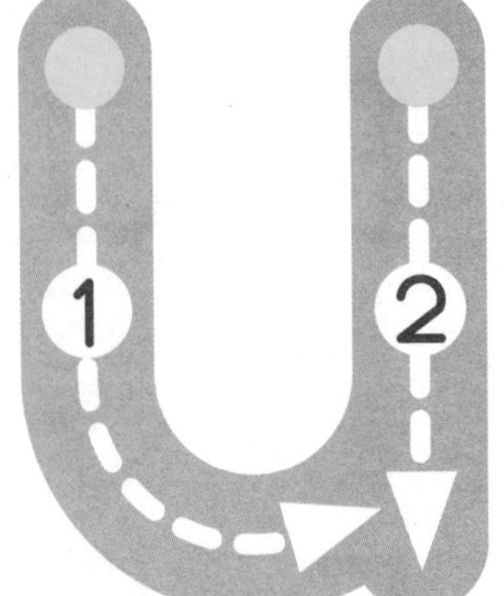

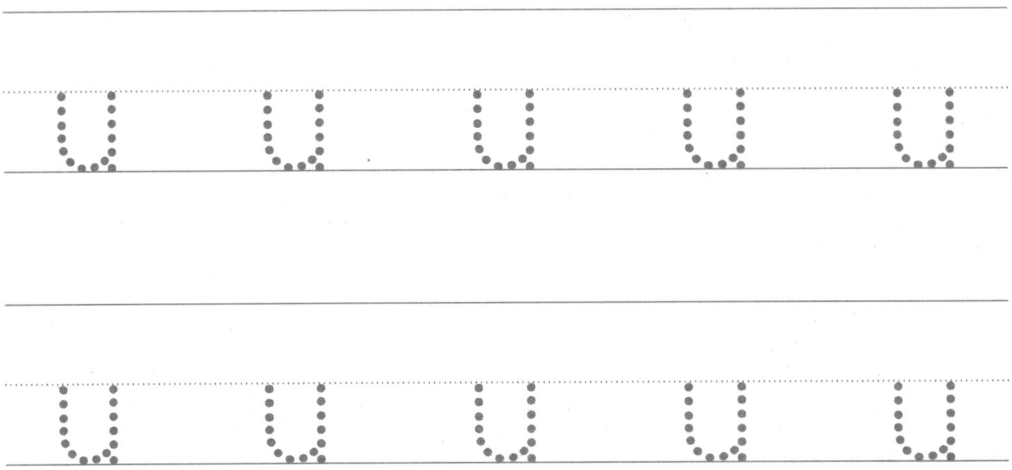

Color the letter v and the vase brightly.

vase

Trace the letter.

v v v v v

v v v v v

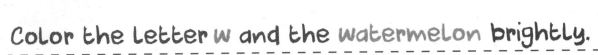

Color the letter w and the watermelon brightly.

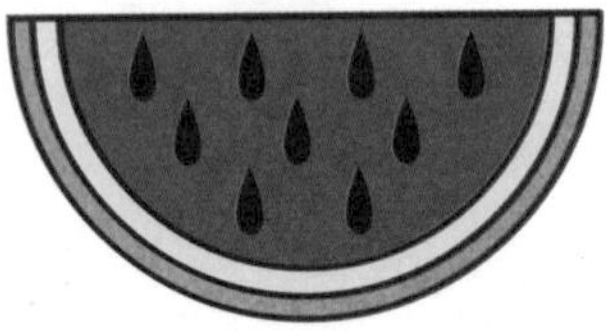

watermelon

Trace the letter.

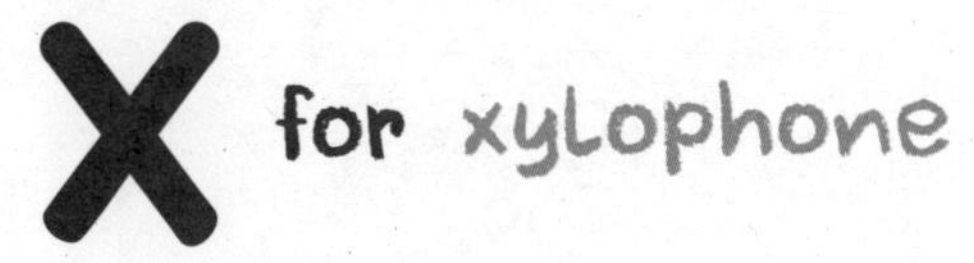

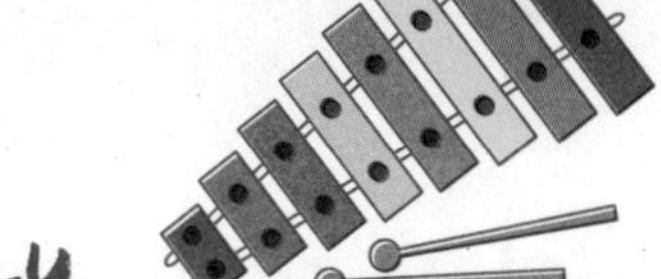

Color the letter x and the xylophone brightly.

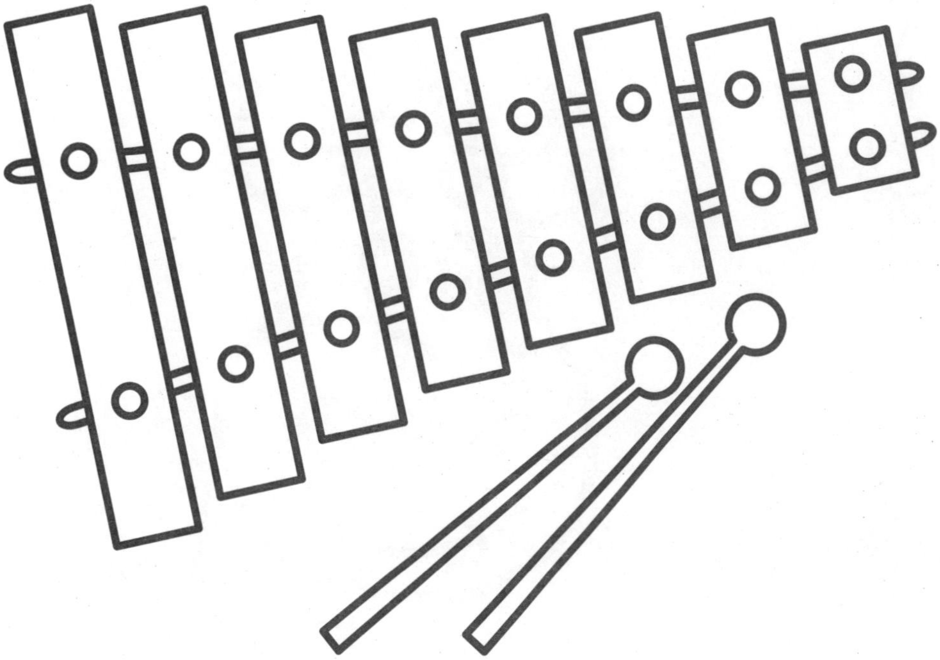

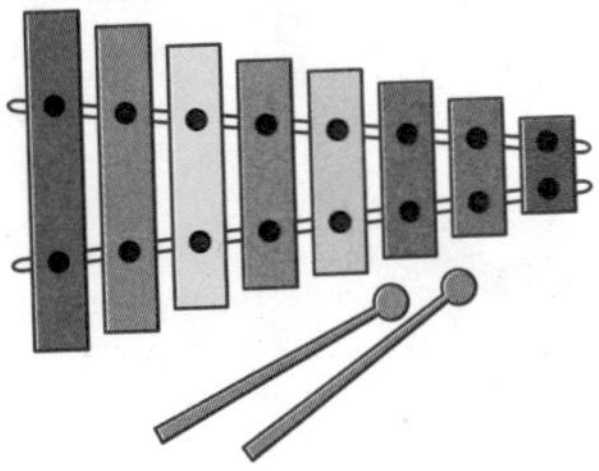

xylophone

Trace the letter.

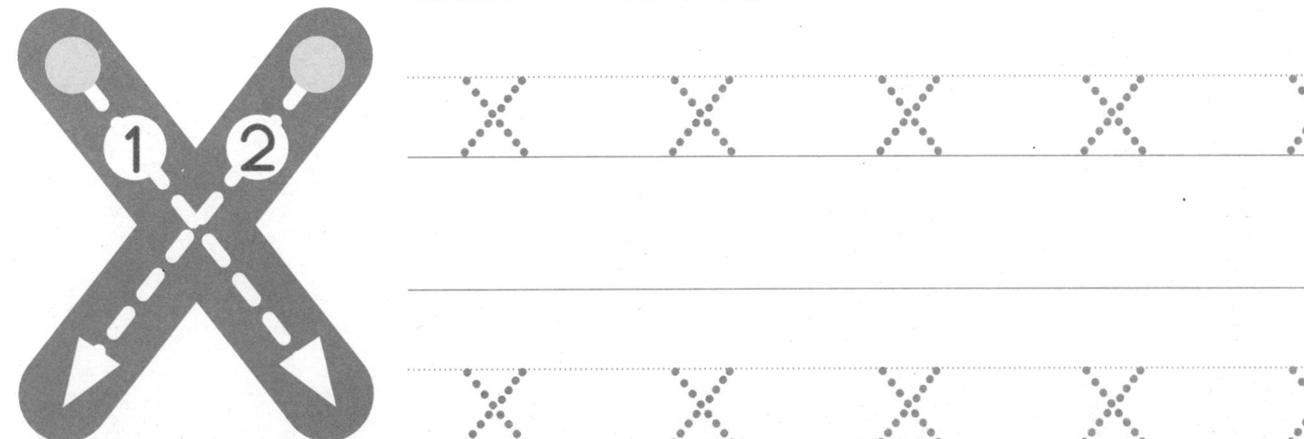

y for yak

Color the letter y and the yak brightly.

y

yak

Trace the letter.

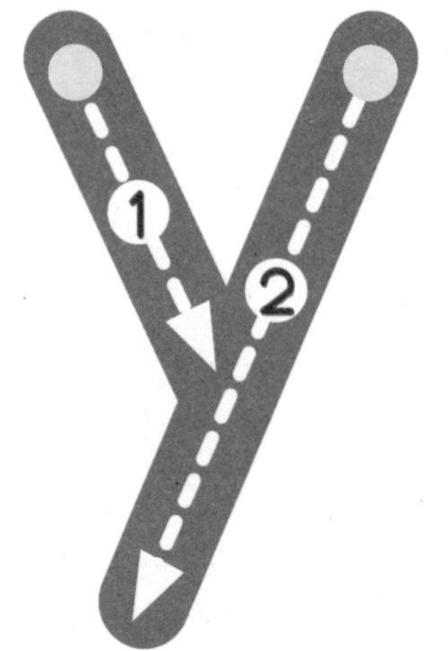

y y y y y

y y y y y

Z for zebra

Color the letter z and the zebra brightly.

zebra

Trace the letter.

Match Them Up!

Trace the given letters and match with the correct picture.

Find the First Letter!

Circle the beginning letter of each picture.

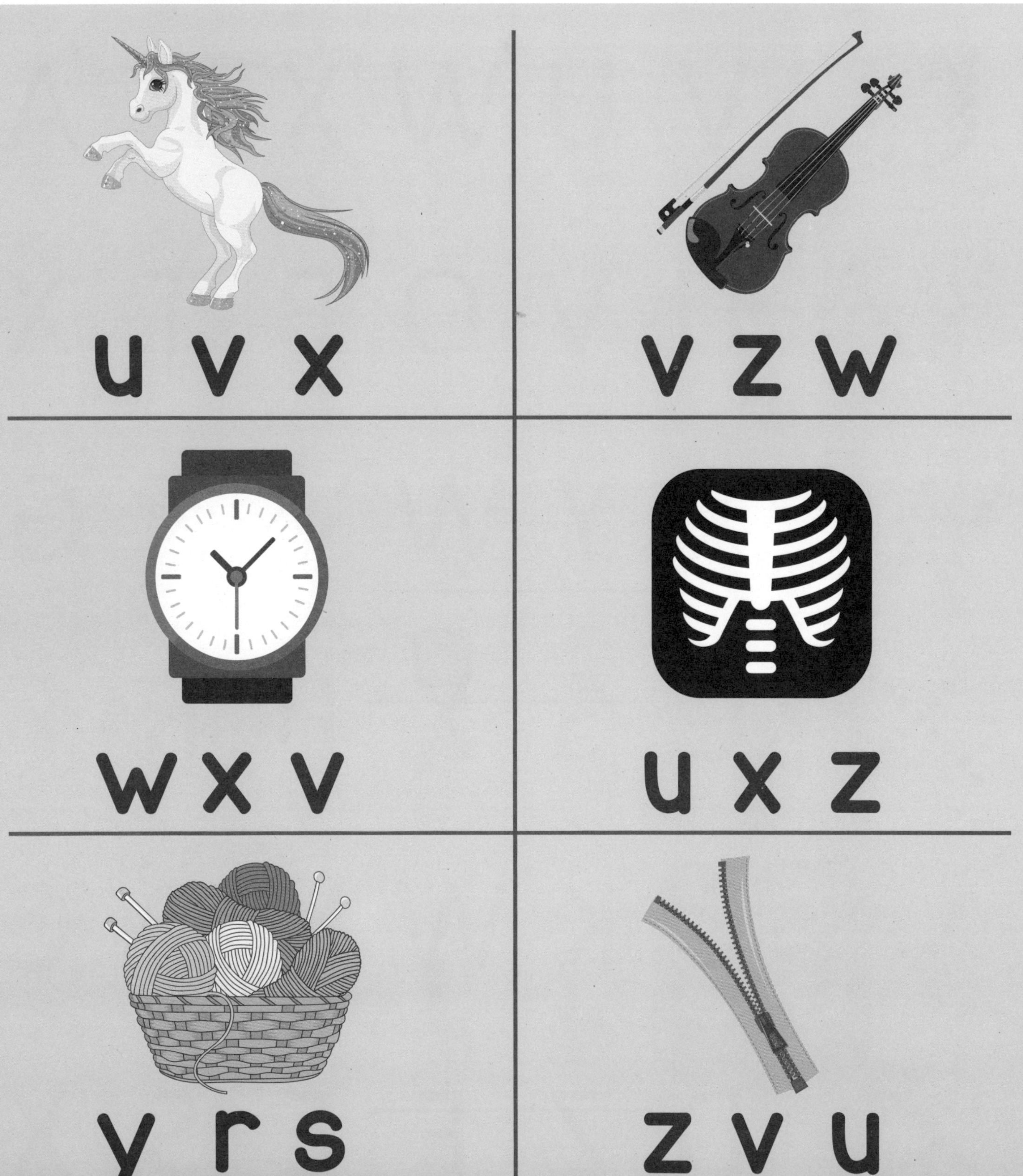

Circle the Matching Letter!

Trace and match the Lowercase Letter with its Uppercase Letter in each row.

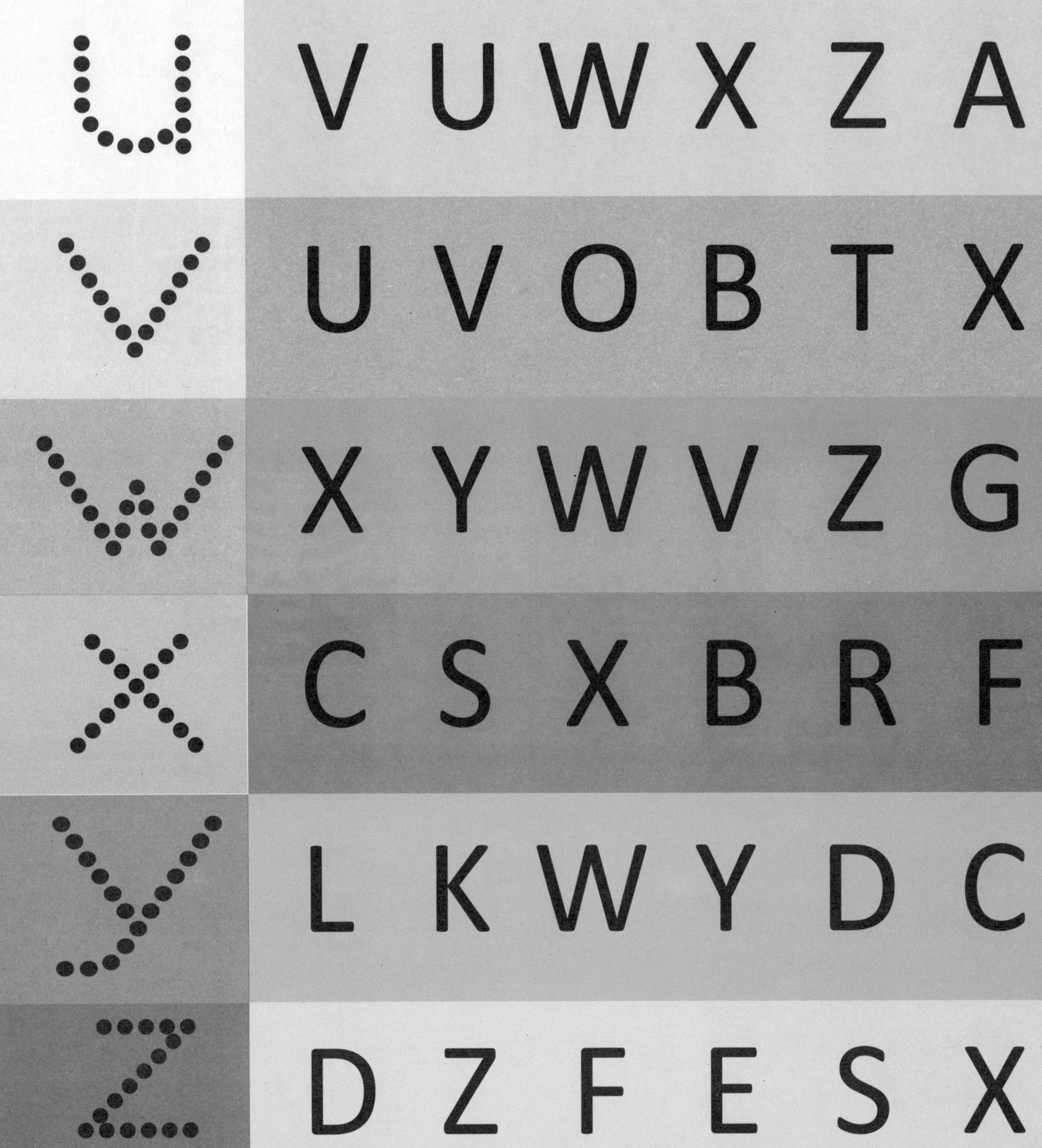

abc Maze!

Draw a line along the abc path till z and take the kitten to its favorite food.

Let's See if You Remember!

Trace the lowercase and uppercase letters of the alphabet and say them aloud.

Write the Missing Letters!

Fill the blanks with the missing letters.

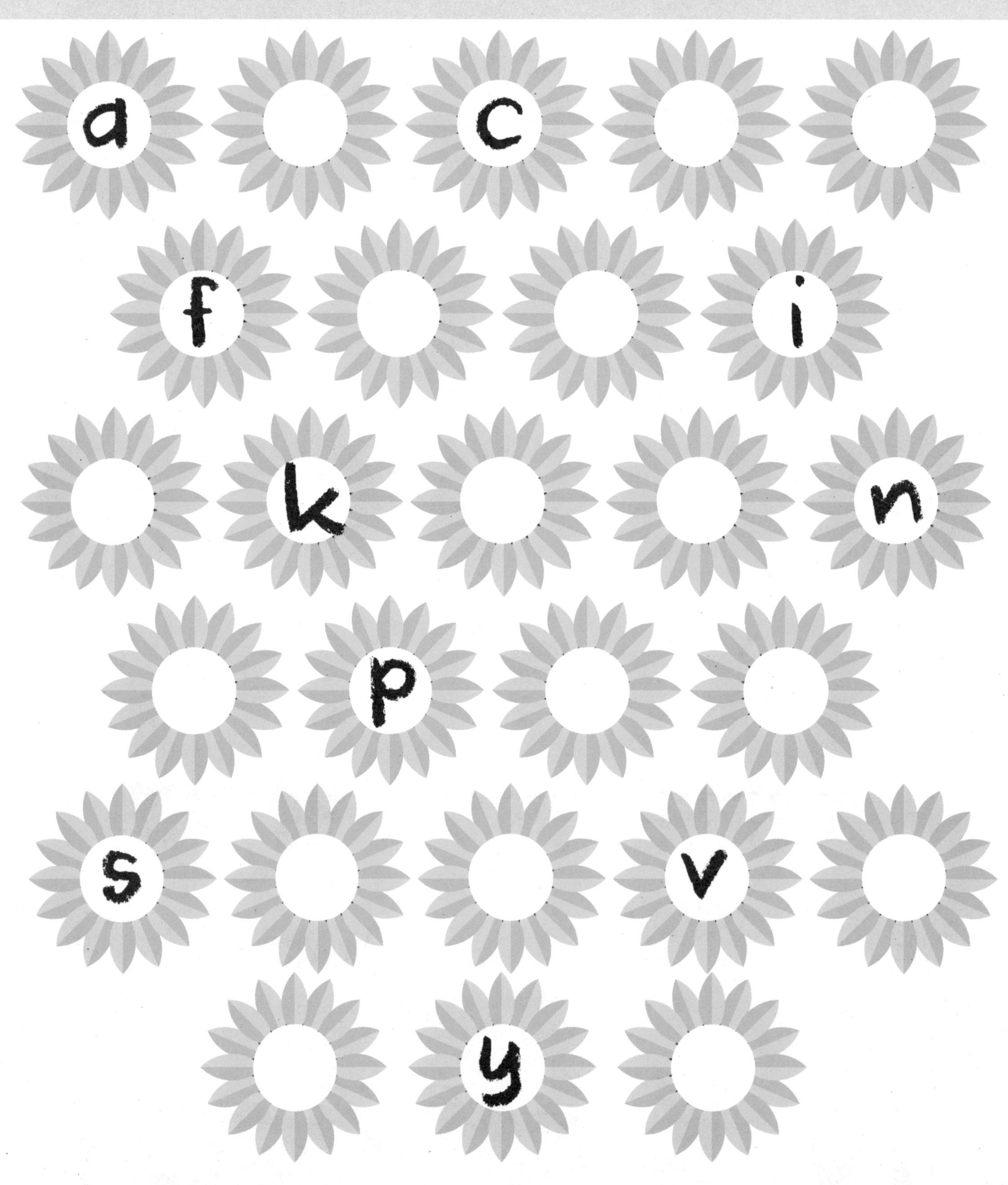

ANSWERS

Match Them Up!

Trace the given letters and match with the correct picture.

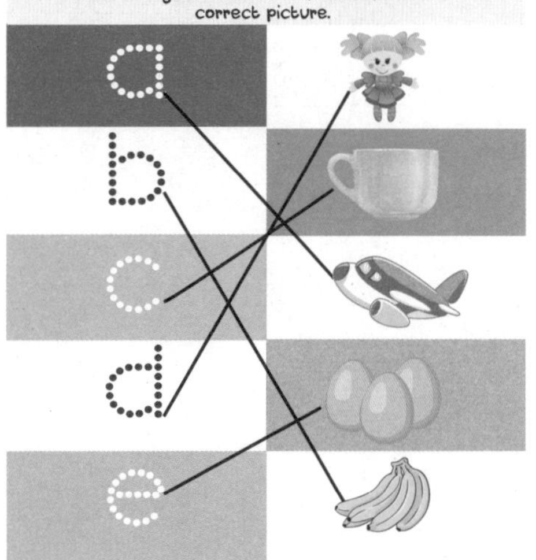

Find the First Letter!

Circle the beginning letter for each picture.

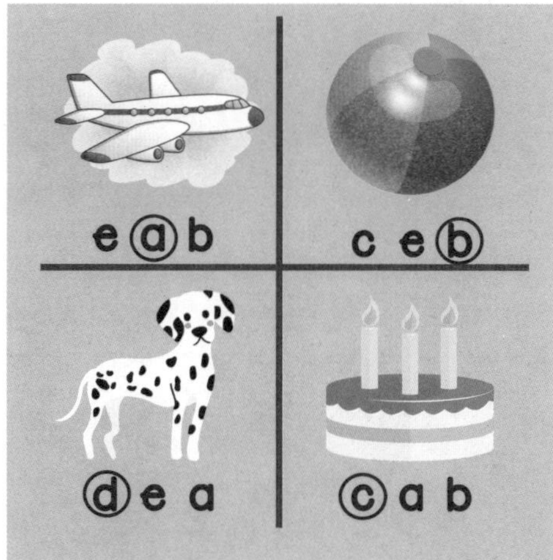

Circle the Matching Letter!

Trace and match the lowercase letter with its Uppercase letter in each row.

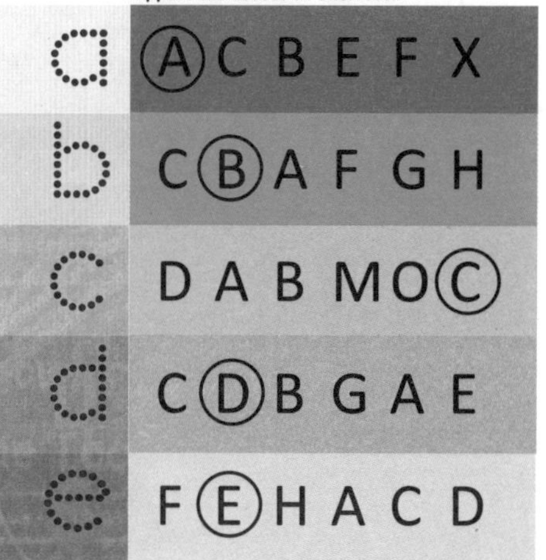

a A C B E F X
b C B A F G H
c D A B M O C
d C D B G A E
e F E H A C D

Match Them Up!

Trace the given letters and match with the correct picture.

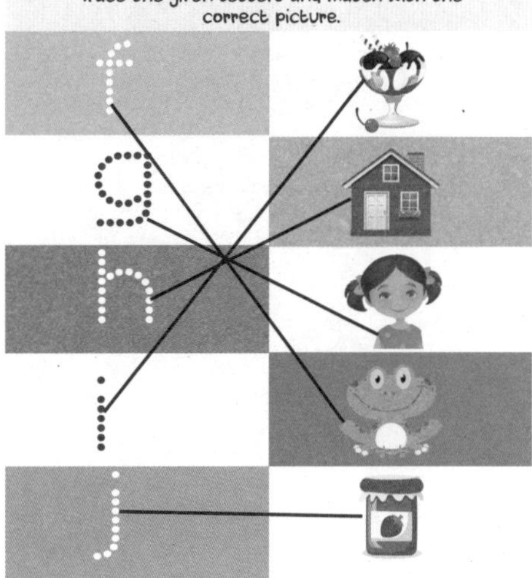

Find the First Letter!

Circle the beginning letter for each picture.

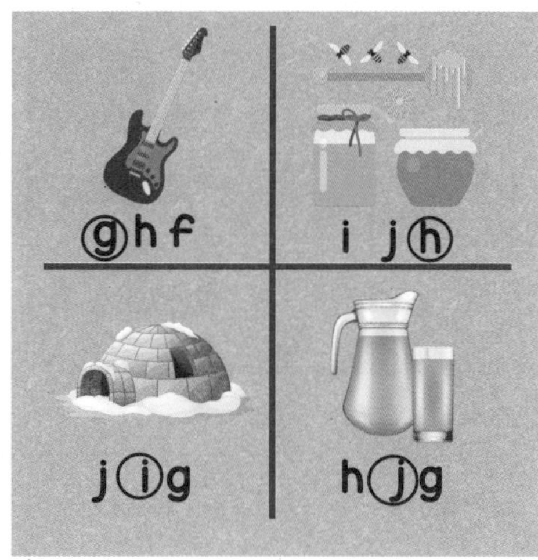

Circle the Matching Letter!

Trace and match the lowercase letter with its Uppercase letter in each row.

f F G H E A J

g A H G B C D

h H D O N P X

i G I D C A S

j H U T J G F

Match Them Up!

Trace the given letters and match with the correct picture.

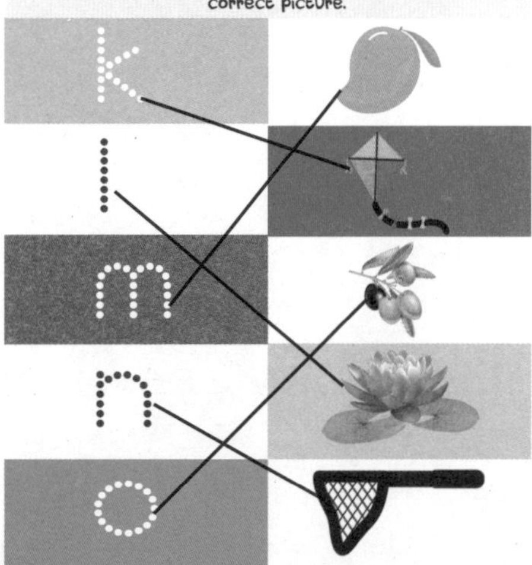

Find the First Letter!

Circle the beginning letter for each picture.

Circle the Matching Letter!

Trace and match the lowercase letter with its Uppercase letter in each row.

k A V K X V G

l L O H J C A

m N M O J W R

n M B N Z A S

o D O P Q G S

ANSWERS

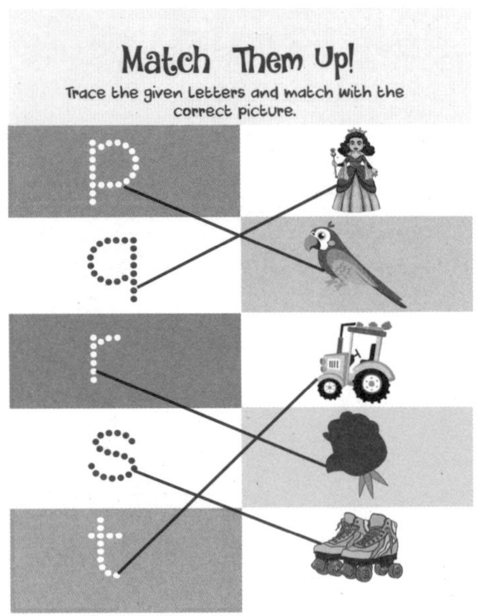

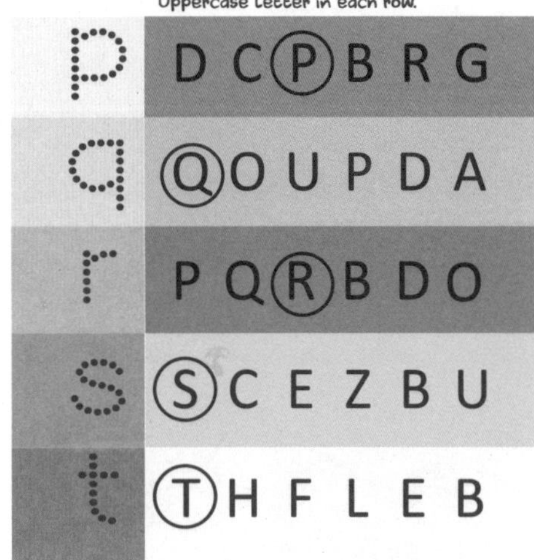

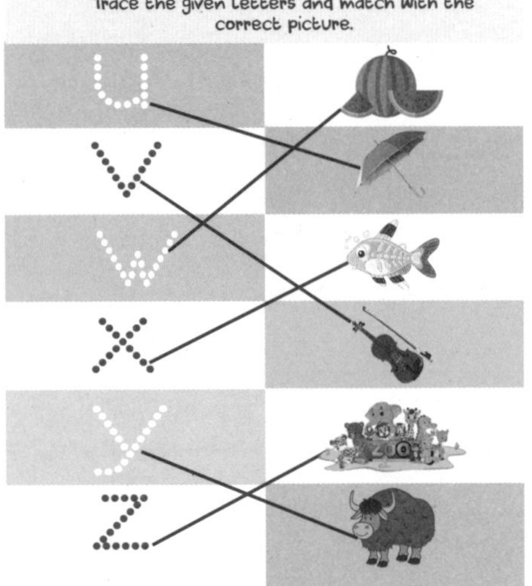

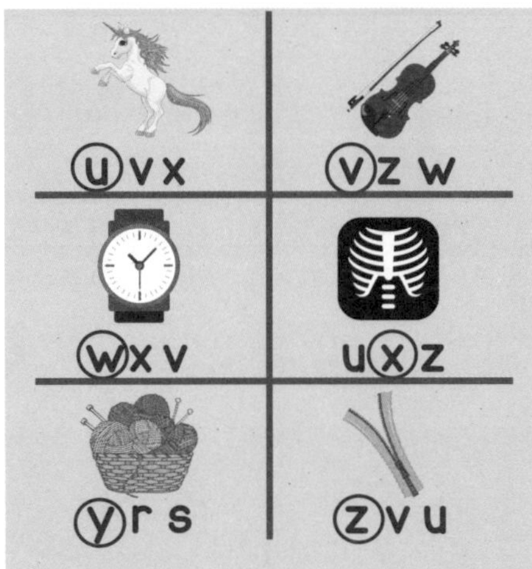

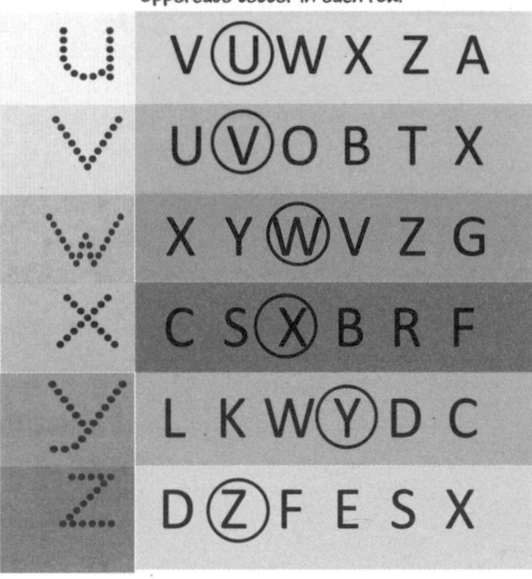

Write the Missing Letters!

Fill the blanks with the missing letters.

a b c d e

f g h i

j k l m n

o p q r

s t u v w

x y z

My First Book Of Patterns

Numbers

1 TO 20

With Coloring and Illustrated Activities

one

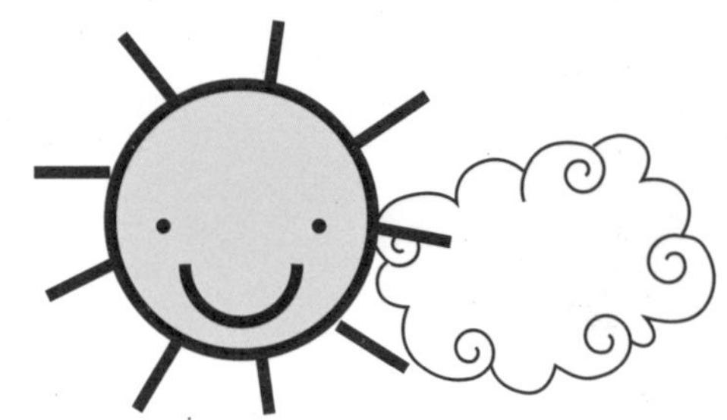

Count and color the only sun in the sky.

Trace the number

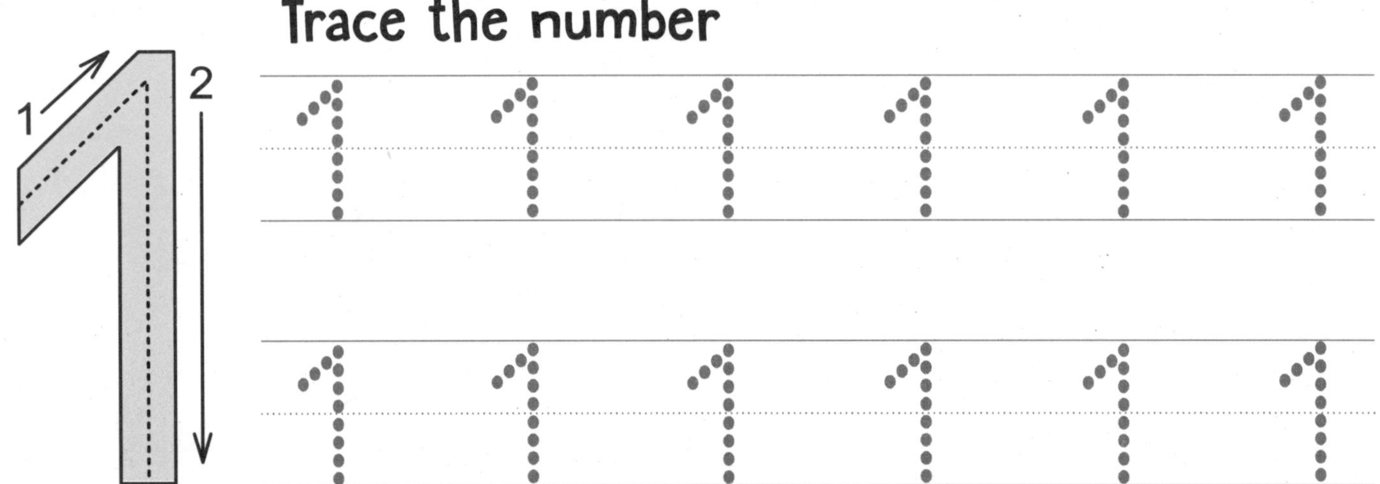

2 two

Count and color the tyres of the bicycle.

Trace the number

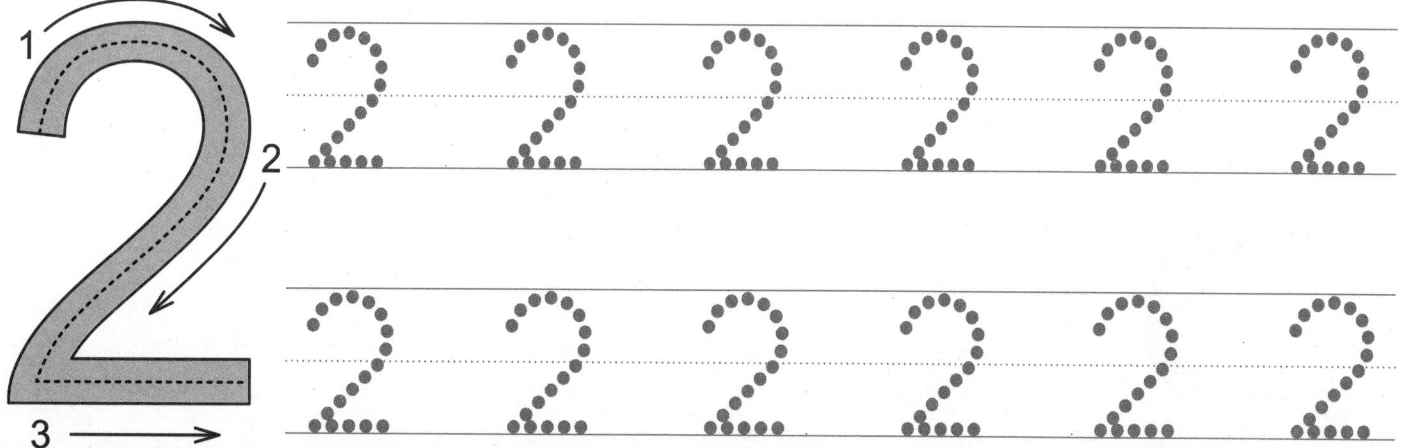

3 three

Count and color the lotus flowers in the pond.

Trace the number

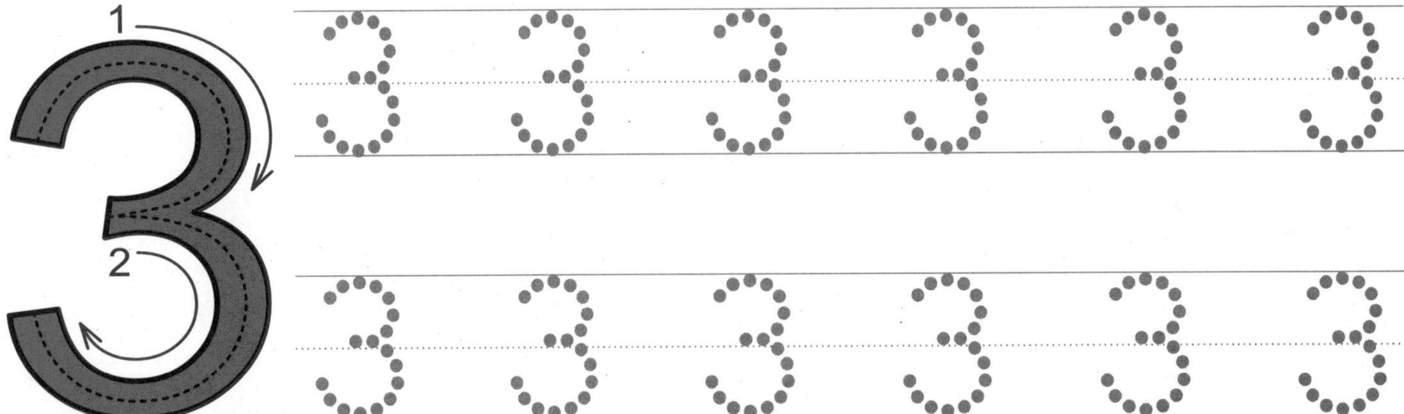

4 four

Count and color the bird houses.

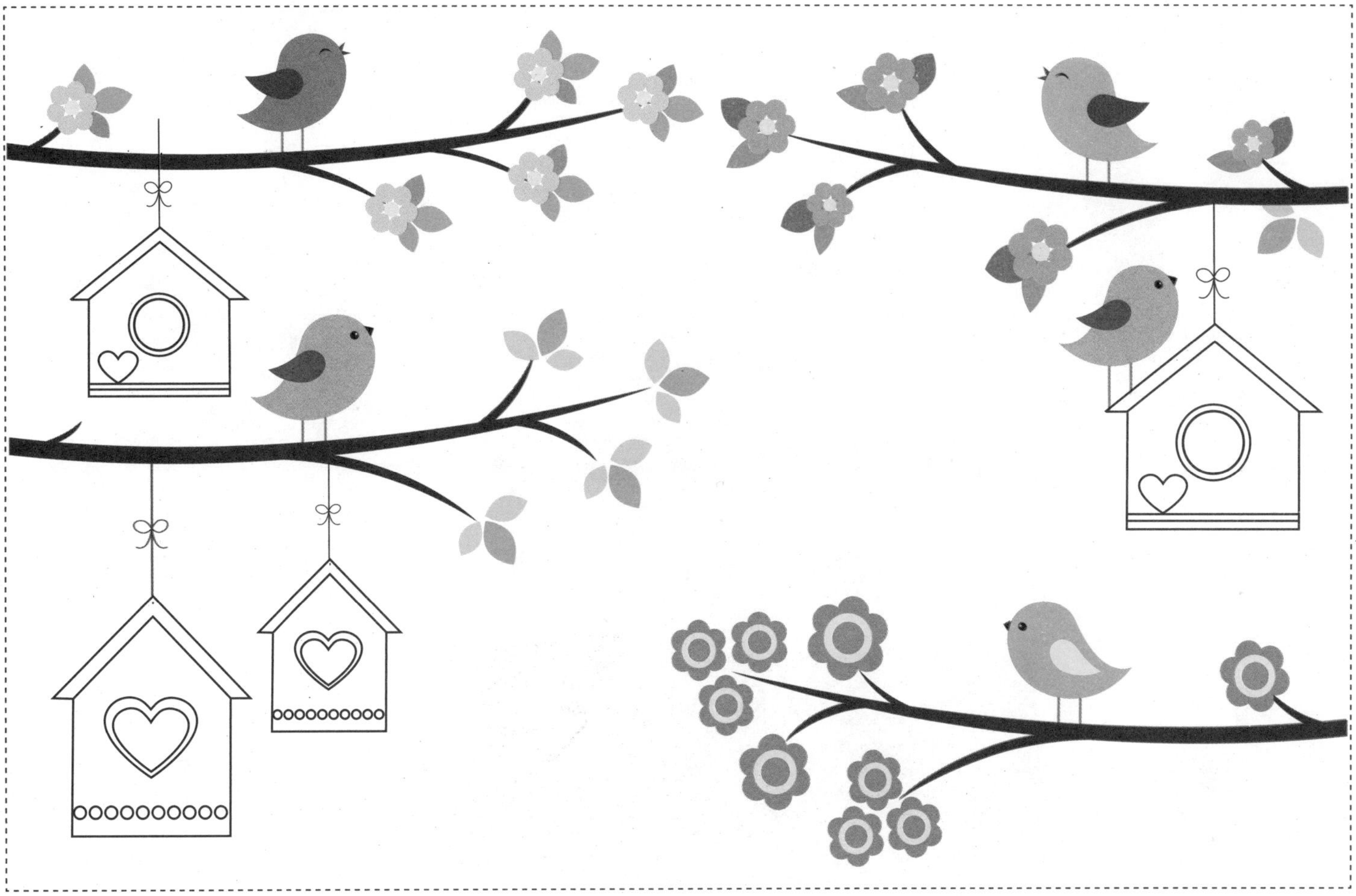

Trace the number

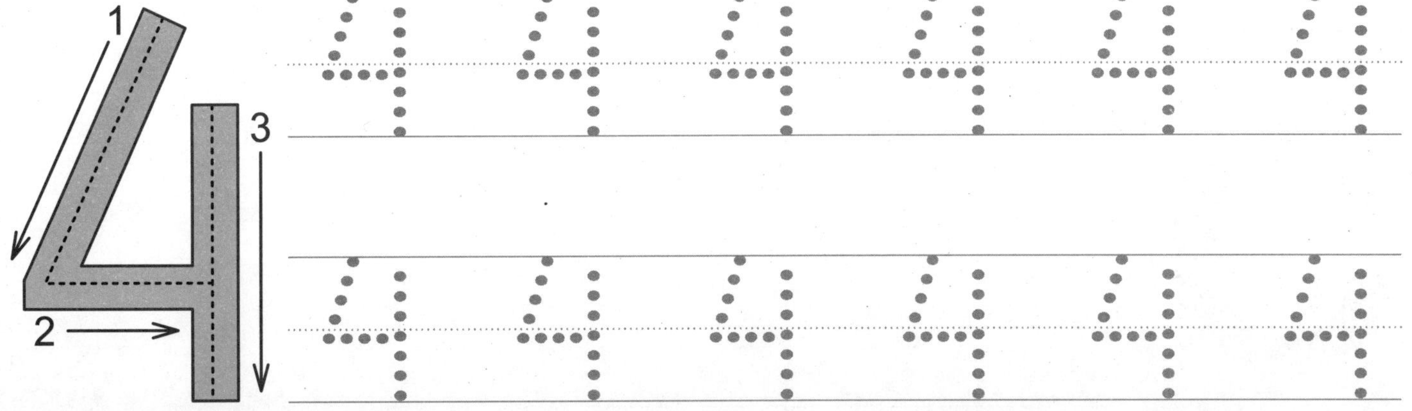

5 five

Count and color the candles on the cake.

Trace the number

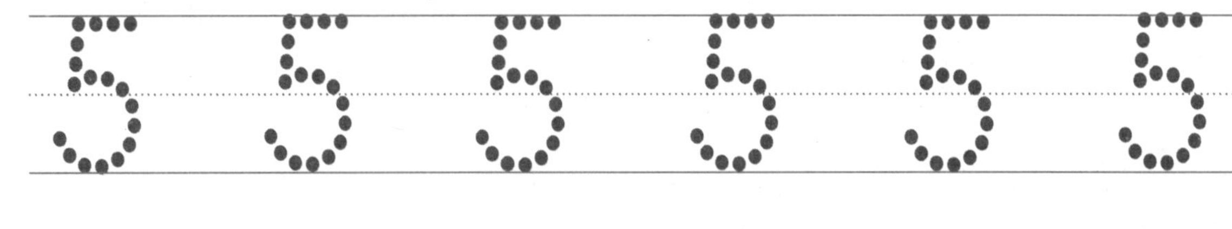

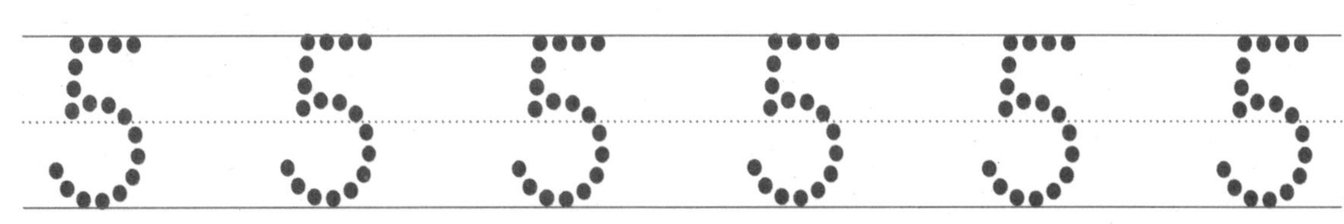

Match Them!

Trace the numbers and match with the correct group of items.

In the Farm

Count the things you see in the farm. Write their correct numbers in the boxes given below with their pictures.

F
G
H
I
J
Answer: A1, B2, C3, D5, E5, F5, G3, H3, I4, J2.

Farm Count

Count and write the number of items in each box.

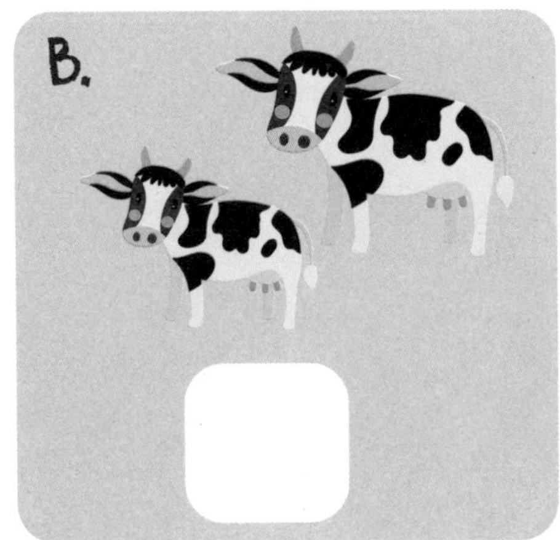

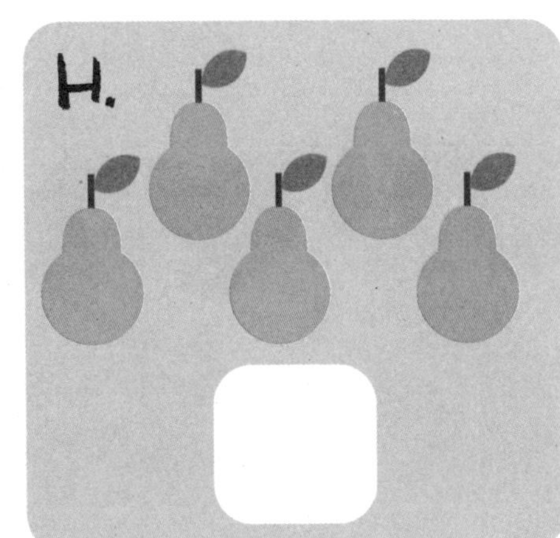

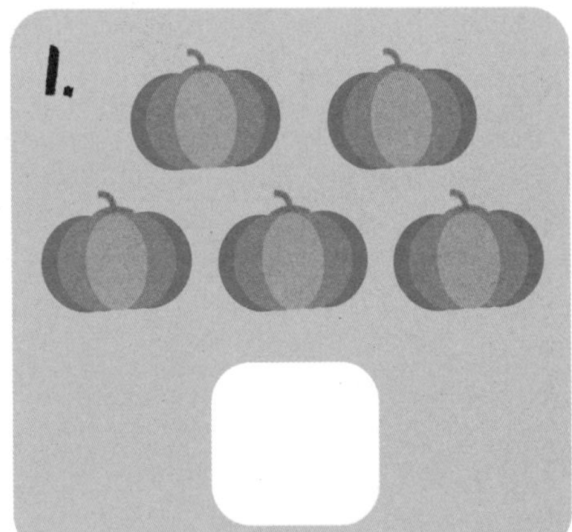

Answer : A 1, B 2, C 3, D 4, E 3, F 4, G 2, H 5, I 5.

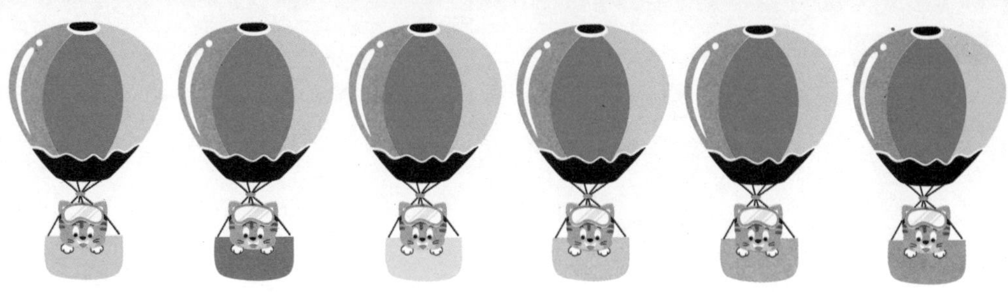

Count and color the hot-air balloons in the sky.

Trace the number

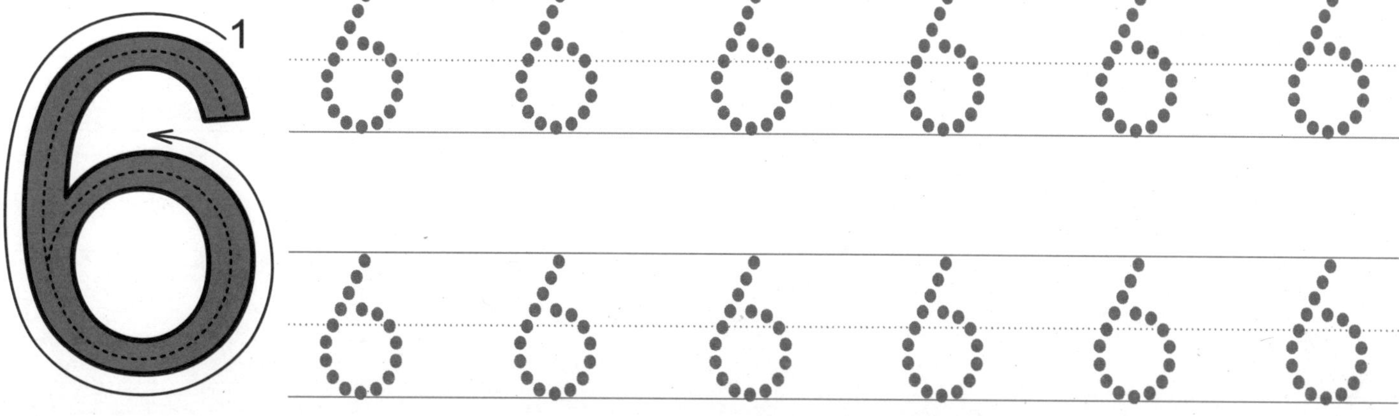

7 seven

Count and fill the colors in the rainbow.

Trace the number

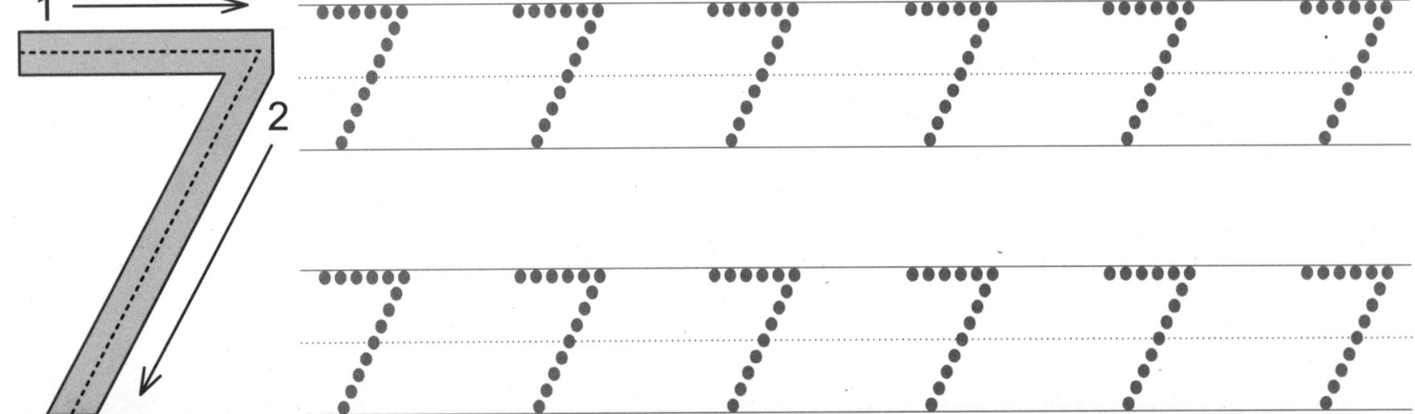

8 eight

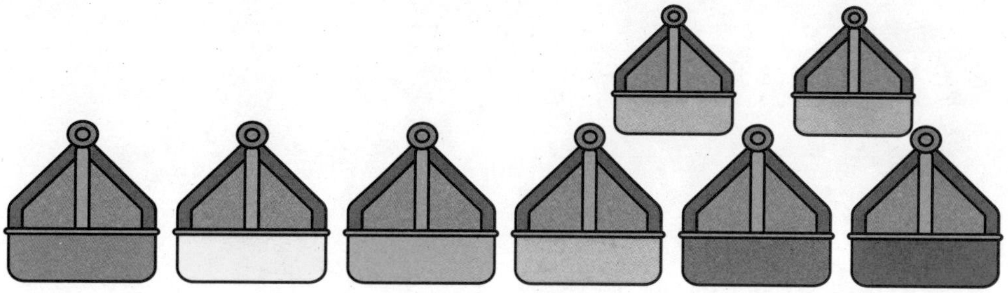

Trace the numbers on the carts of the giant wheel.

1 2 3 4 5 6 7 8

Trace the number

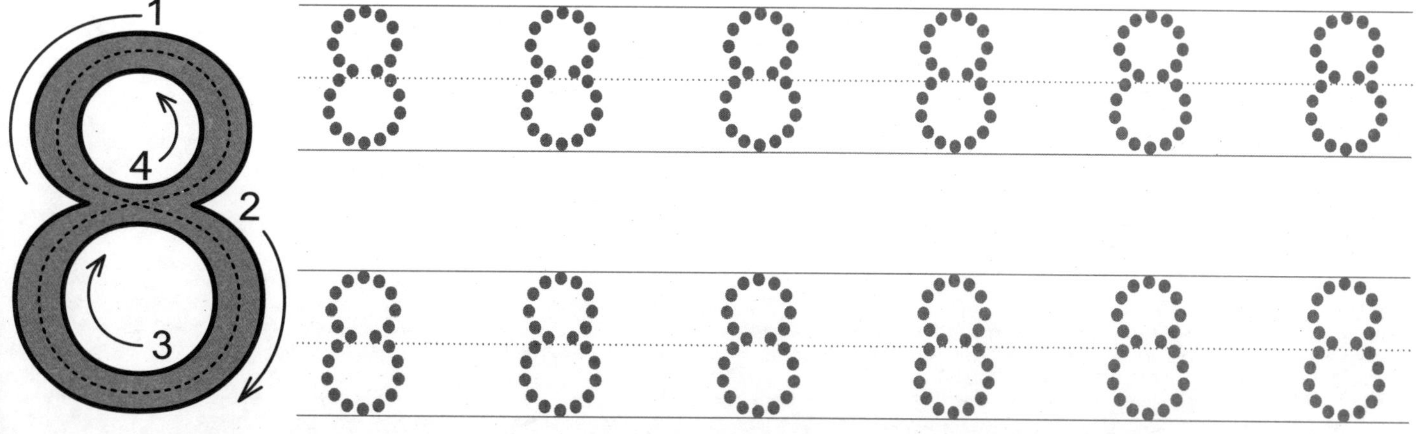

9 nine

Count and color the ducks in the pond.

Trace the number

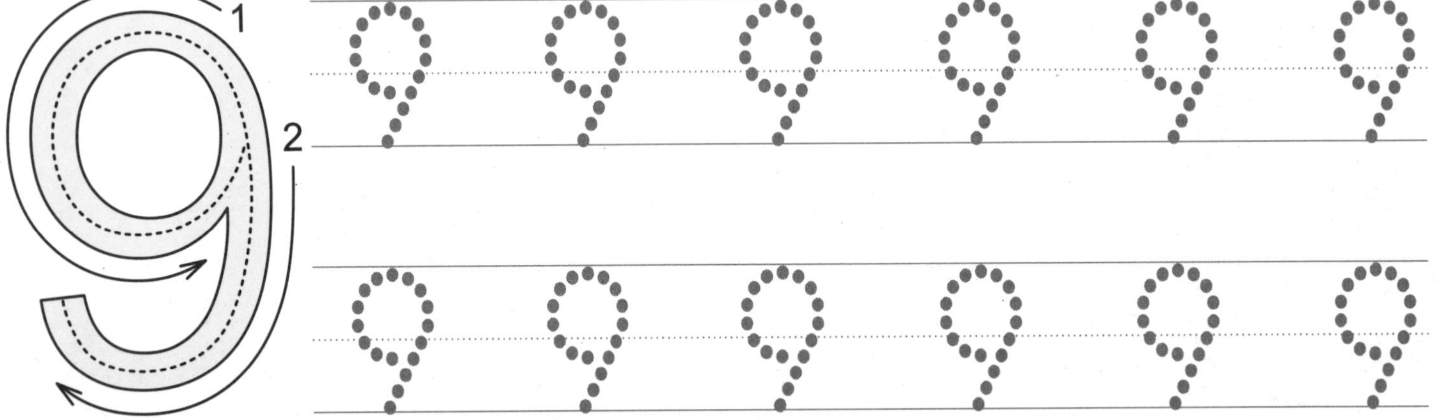

10 ten

Count and color the lollipops.

Trace the number

At the Zoo

Count the animals you see at the Zoo. Write their numbers in the boxes given below with their picture.

F
G
H
I
J
Answer: A 1, B 3, C 4, D 10, E 5, F 8, G 6, H 7, I 12, J 9.

Zoo Count

Count and write the number of animals in each box.

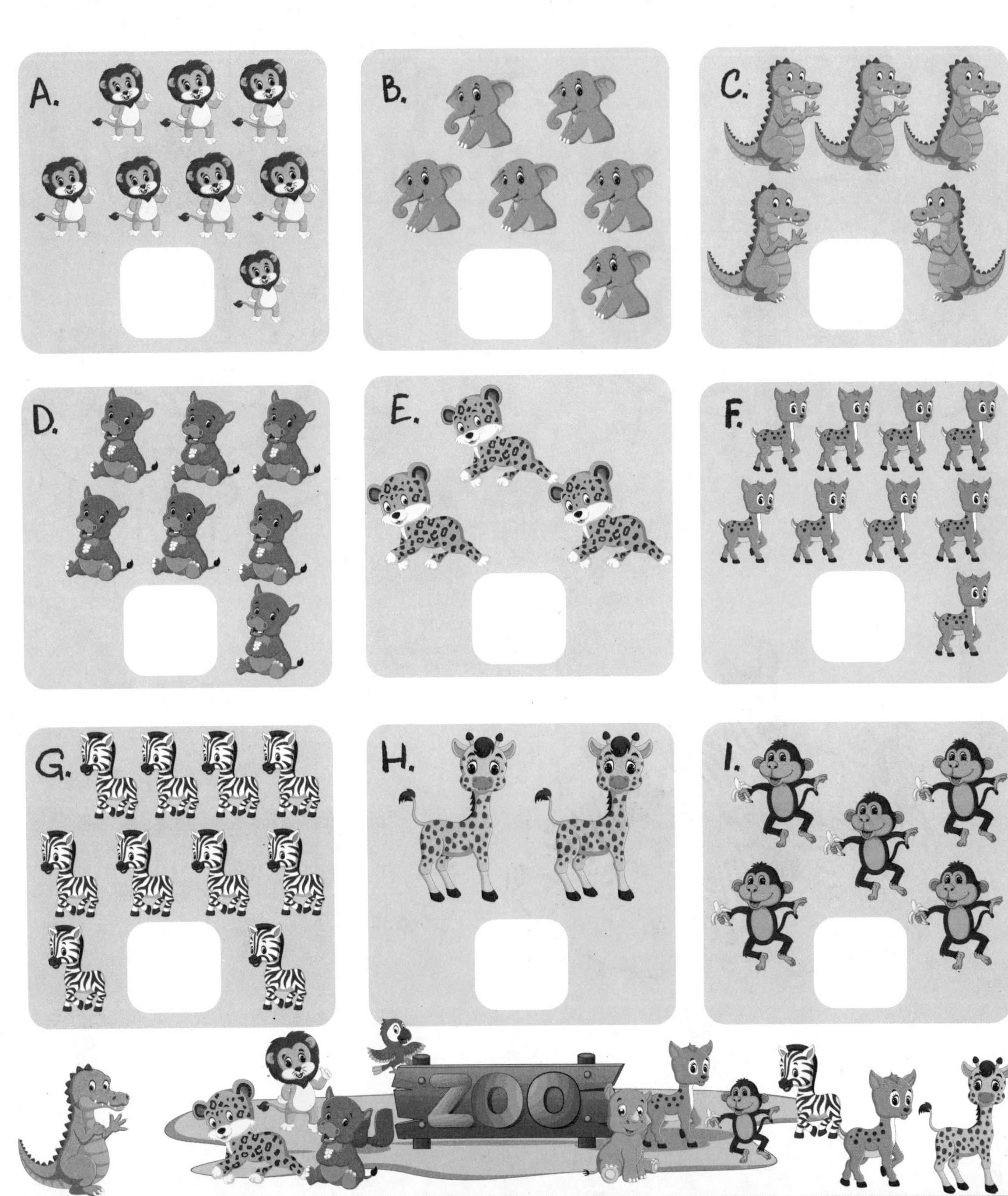

Answer : A 8, B 6, C 5, D 7, E 3, F 9, G 10, H 2, I 5.

Match Them!

Trace the numbers and match with the correct group of items.

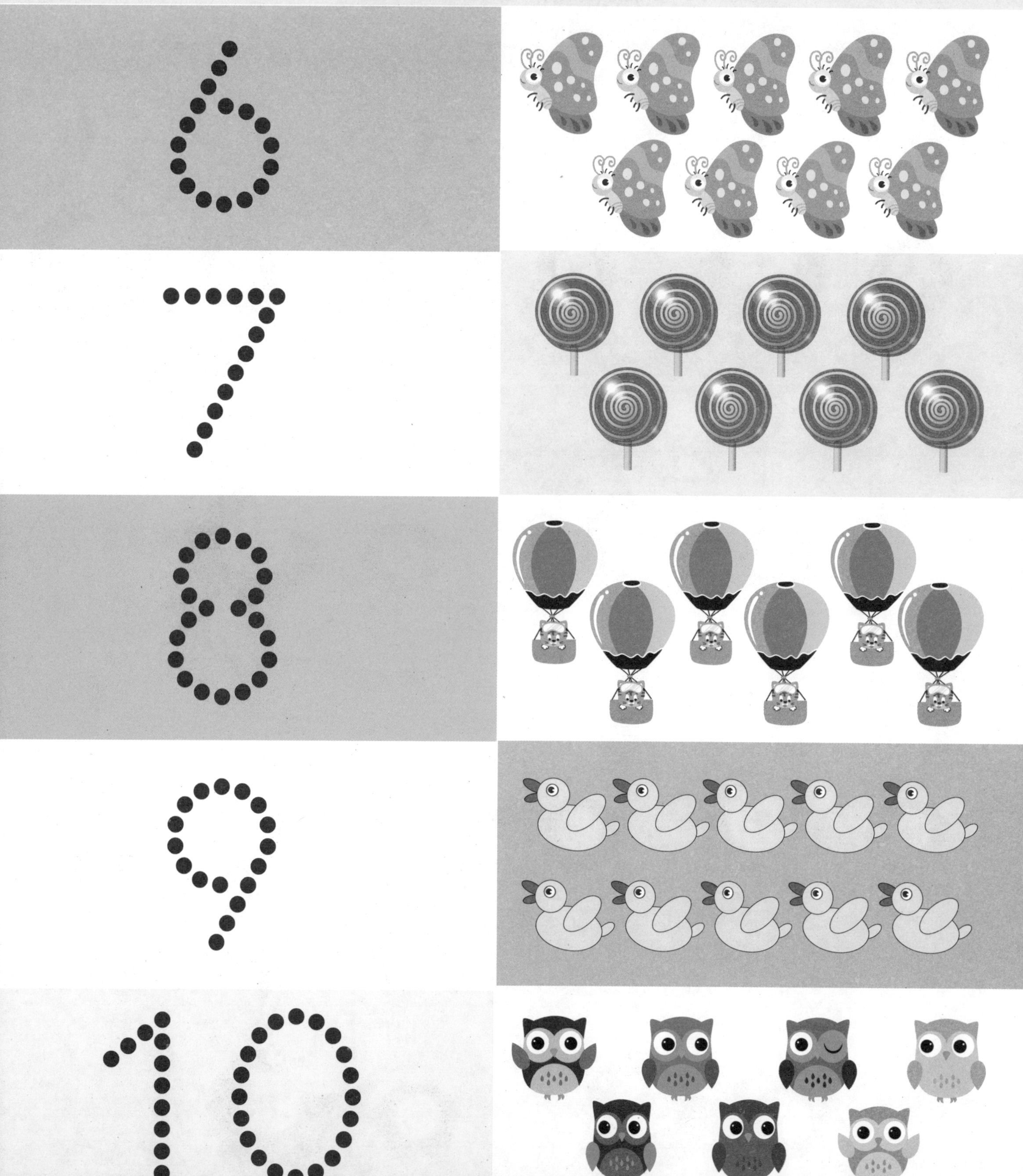

Say Aloud!

Trace the number on each tractor and say their names aloud.

Missing Numbers!

Fill in the blanks to complete the number sequence.

1 ___ 3

3 ___ 5 ___ 7 ___

___ 6 ___ 8 ___ 10

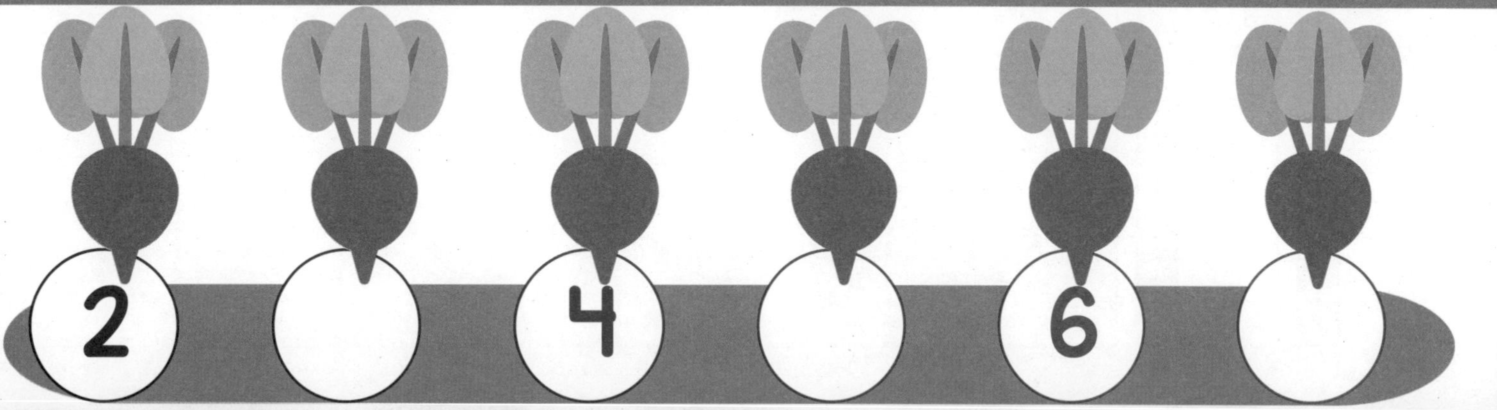

2 ___ 4 ___ 6 ___

11 eleven

Count and color the umbrellas.

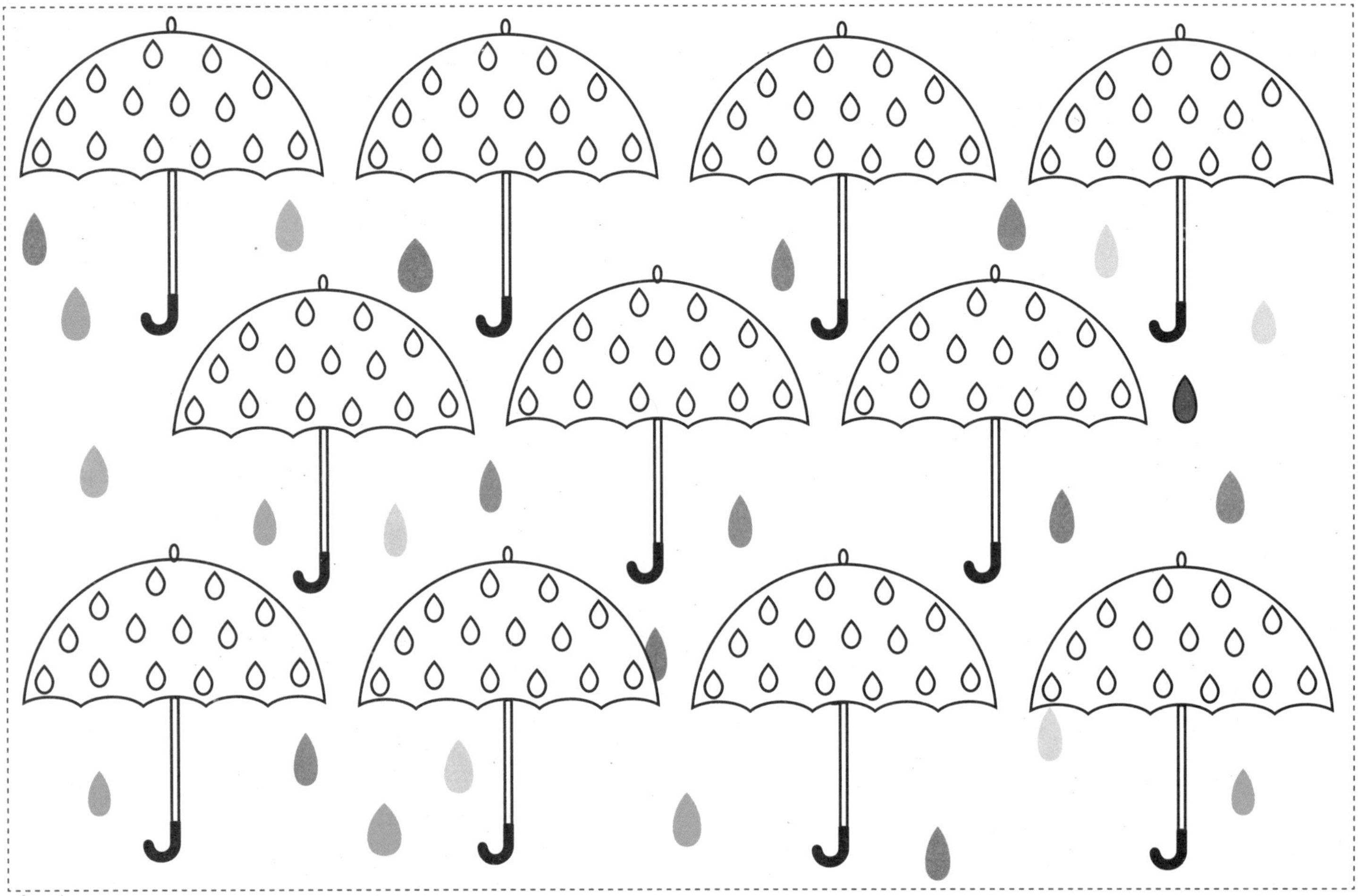

Trace the number

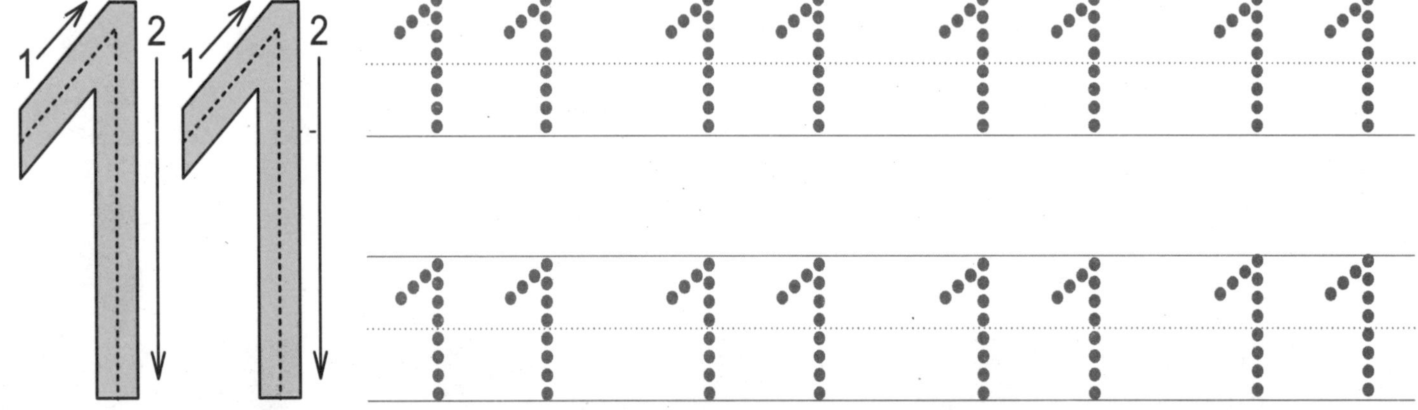

12 twelve

Count and color the ants walking towards the ant hill.

Trace the number

13 thirteen

Count and color the balloons.

Trace the number

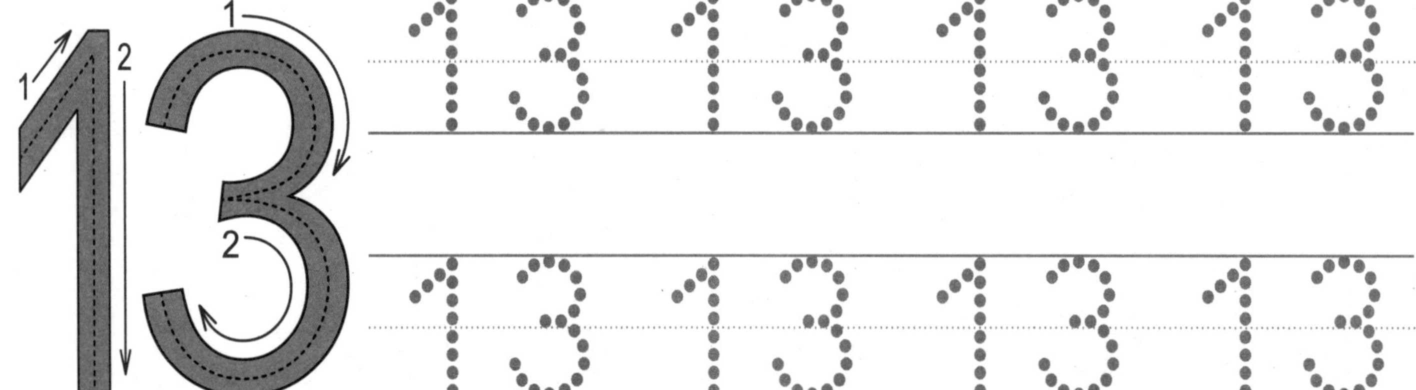

14 fourteen

Count and color the butterflies in the garden.

Trace the number

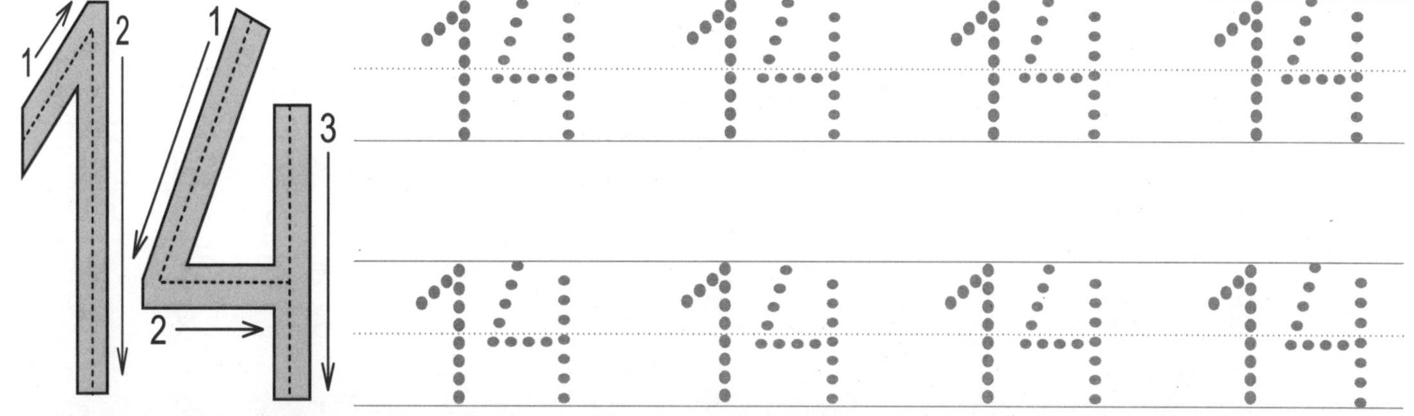

15 fifteen

Count and color the ice creams.

Trace the number

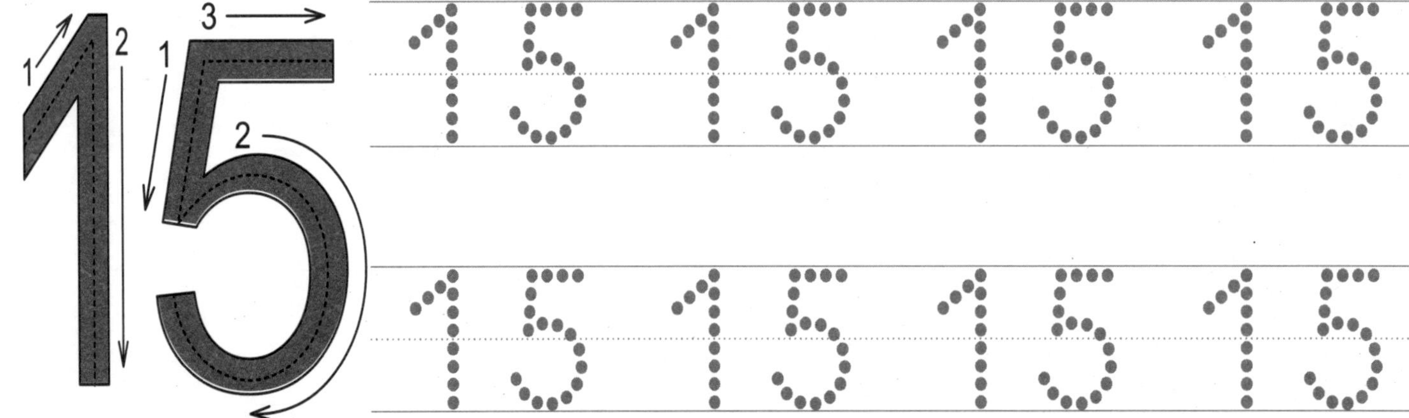

Match Them!

Trace the numbers and match with the correct group of items.

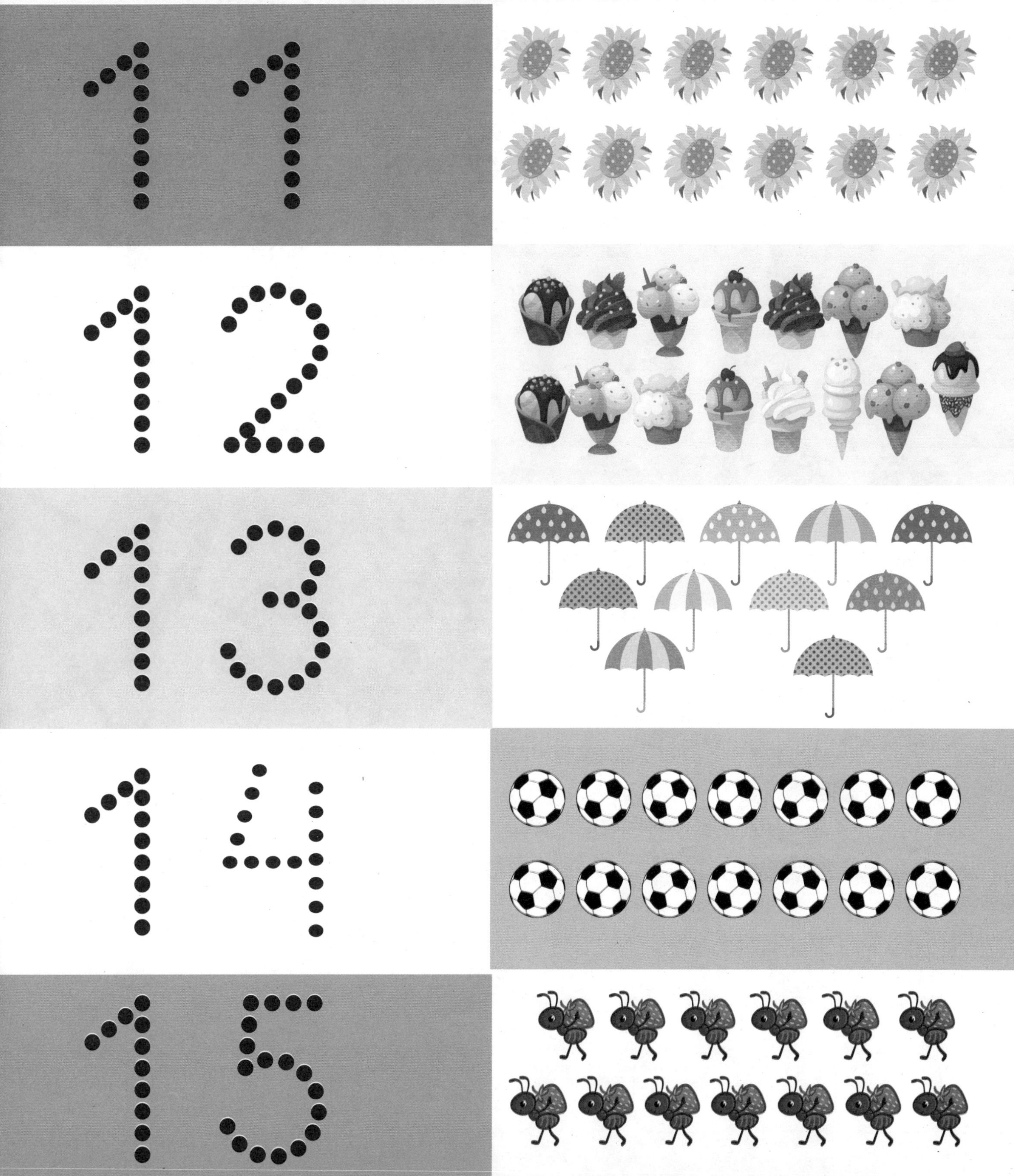

Amusement Park

Count the things you see in the amusement park. Write their correct numbers in the boxes given below with their pictures.

A

B

C

D

E

Answer : A 14, B 14, C 12, D 12, E 12, F 7, G 7, H 12 I 8, J 14.

Go-Karting Track

Rank the winners of the go-karting competition.

First

Second

According to their position in the competition Write the car number in the boxes given below.

Answer : first 13, Second 15, Third 12, Fourth 14, Fifth 11.

16 sixteen

Count and color the ladybirds.

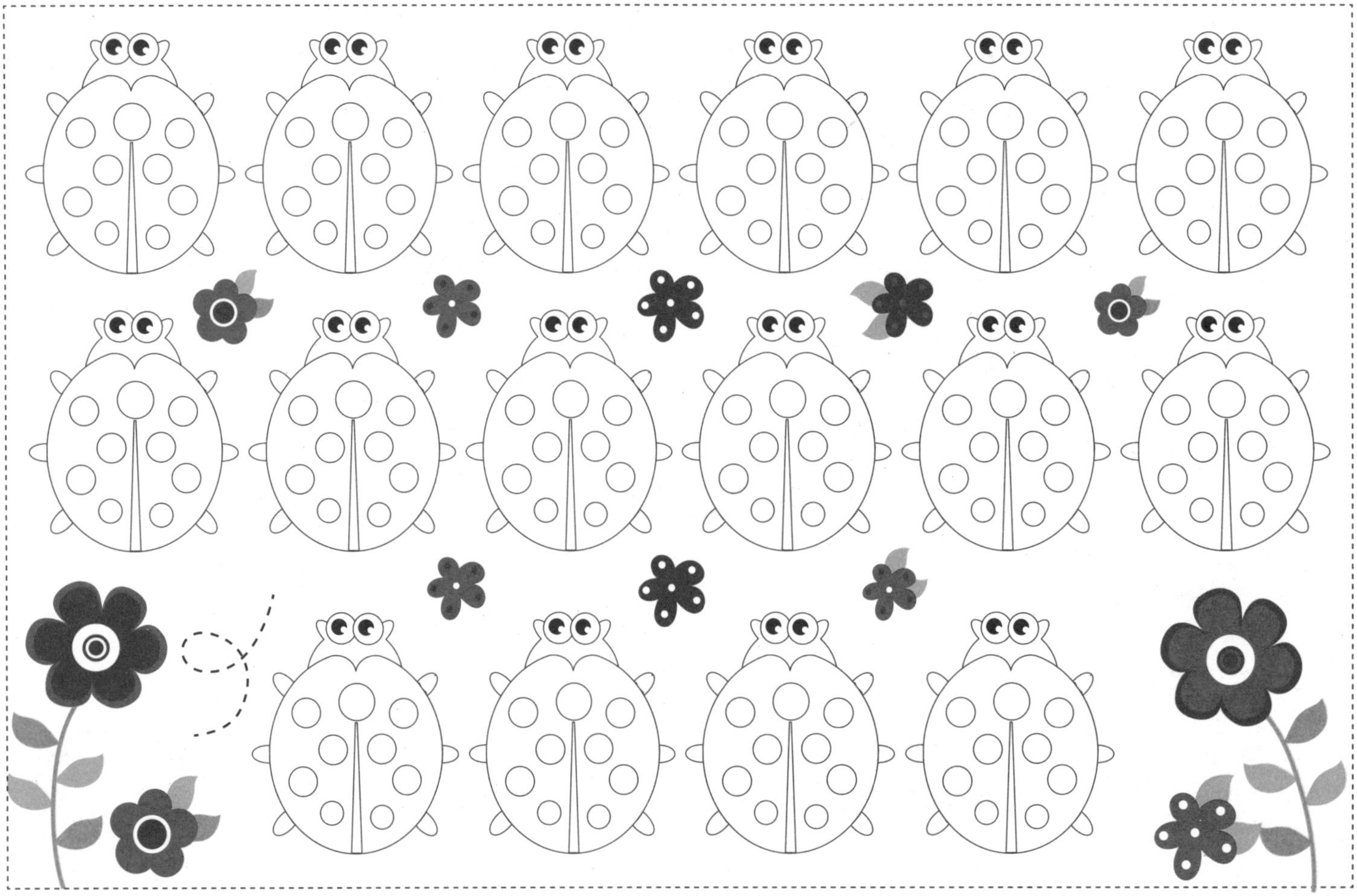

Trace the number

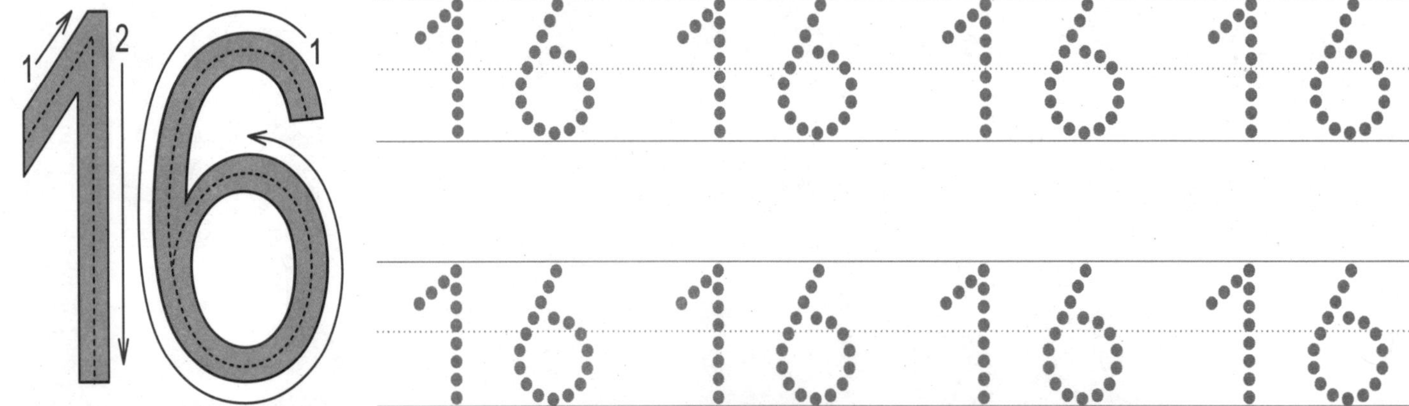

17 seventeen

Count and color the flowers.

Trace the number

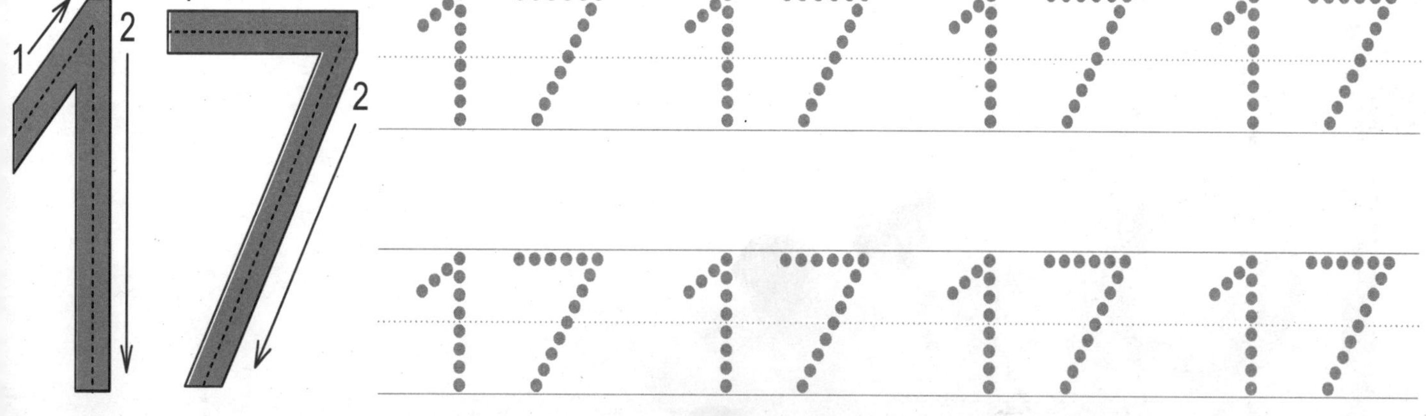

18 eighteen

Count and color the vehicles on the street.

Trace the number

19 nineteen

Count and color the bees.

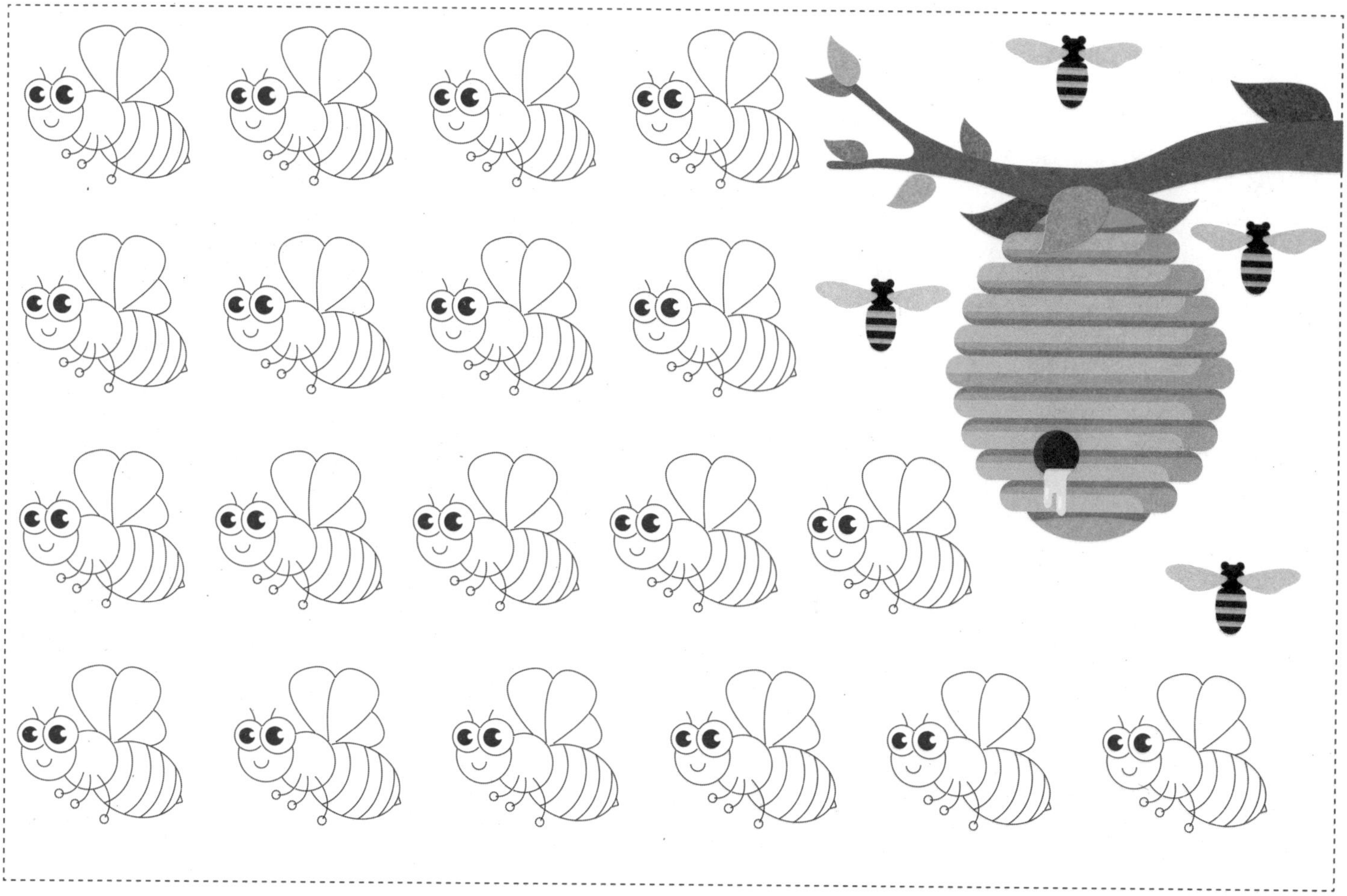

Trace the number

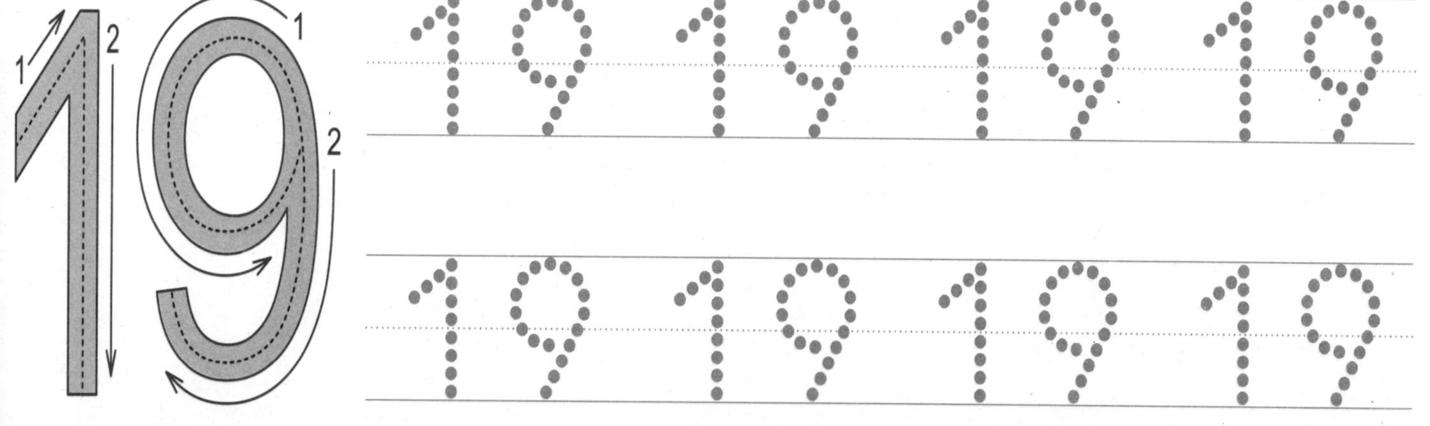

20 twenty

Count and color the stars in the sky.

Trace the number

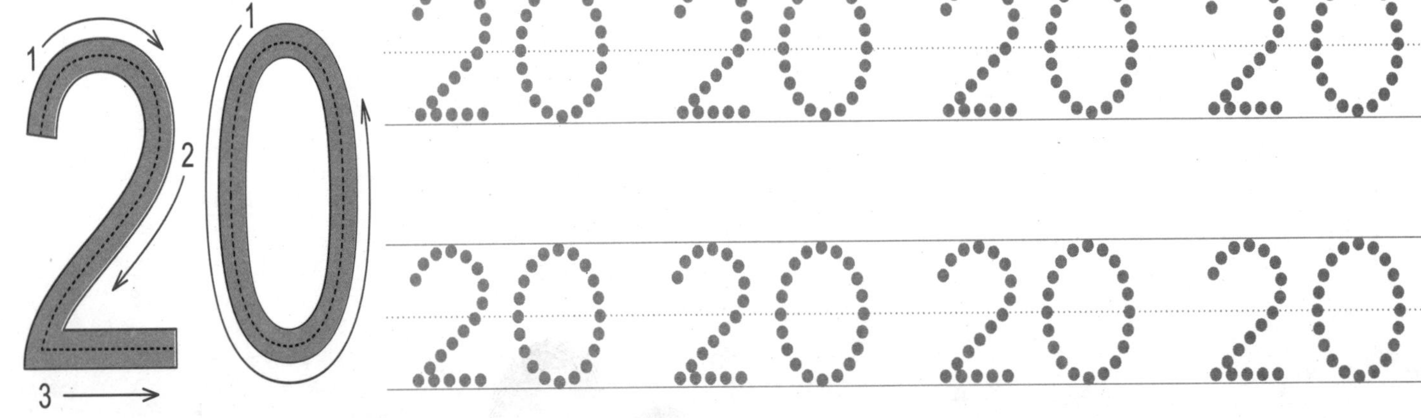

Match Them!

Trace the numbers and match with the correct group of items.

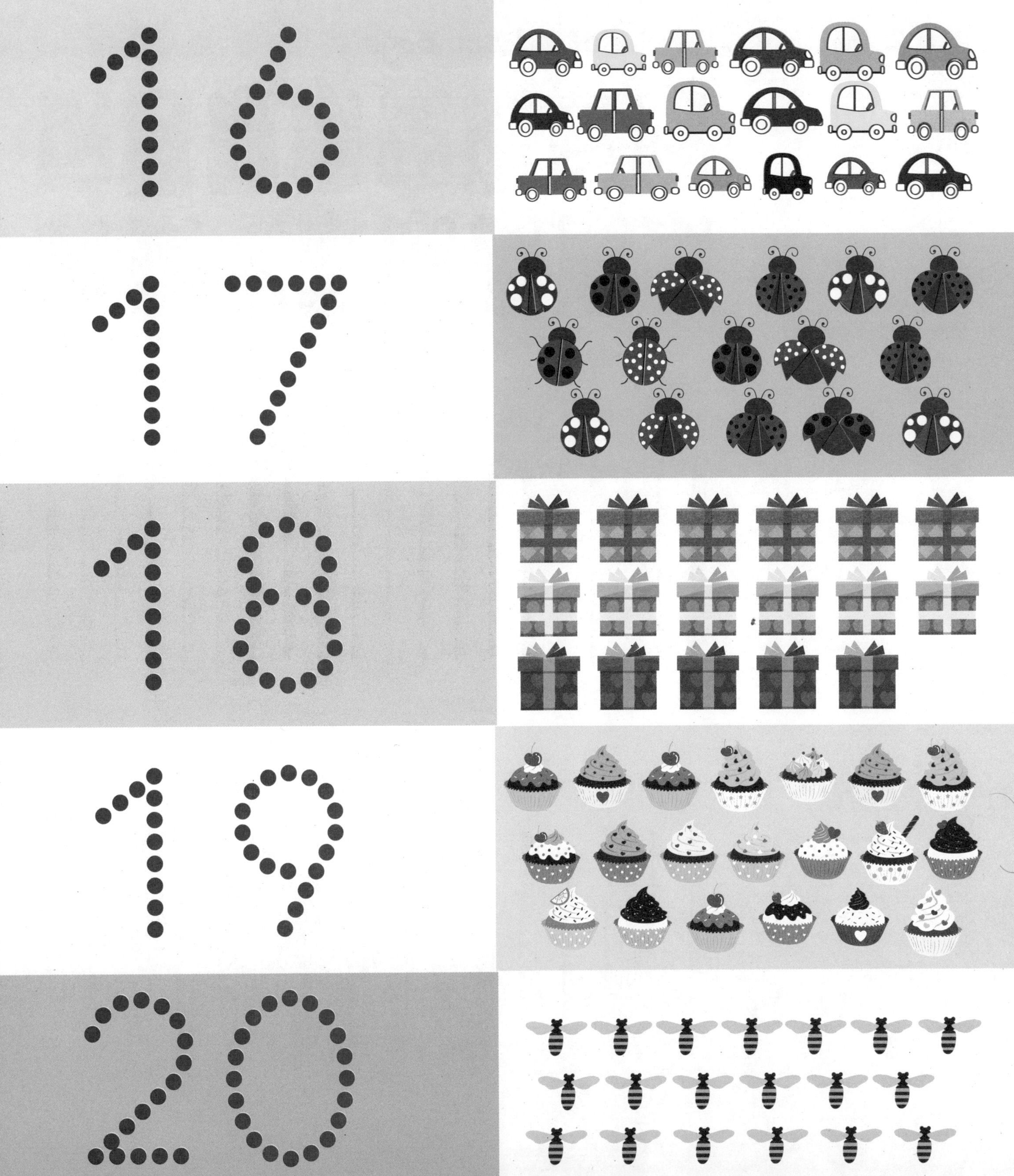

Picture Counting

Count the number of items in each box and color the circle in front of the correct answer.

1. Count the number of school bags.

- A 16
- B 17
- C 19

2. Count the number of color pencils.

- A 16
- B 20
- C 19

3. Count the number of paint brushes.

- A 16
- B 17
- C 19

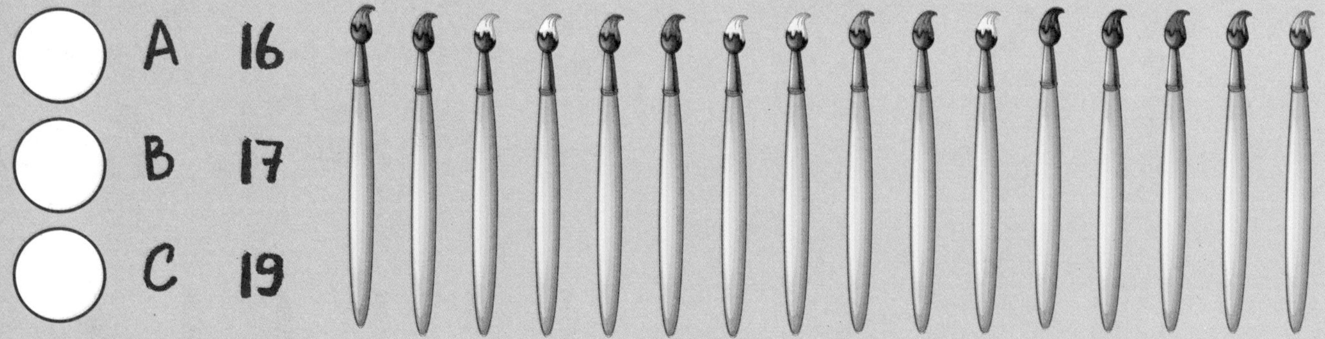

Sharpen your Counting Skills!

4. Count the number of color palettes.

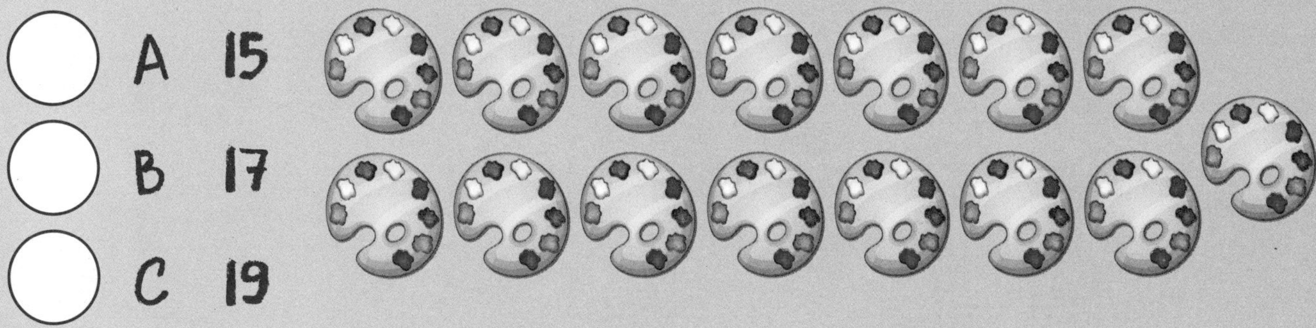

- ◯ A 15
- ◯ B 17
- ◯ C 19

5. Count the number of Water bottles.

- ◯ A 16
- ◯ B 17
- ◯ C 18

6. Count the number of lunch boxes.

- ◯ A 16
- ◯ B 17
- ◯ C 19

Answer : 1 A, 2 B, 3 A, 4 A, 5 C, 6 B.

In the Ocean

Count the things you see under the ocean. Write their correct numbers in the boxes given below with their picture.

A ☐ B ☐ C ☐ D ☐ E ☐

F

G

H

I

J

Answer : A 17, B 14, C 17, D 11, E 9, F 14, G 15, H 13, I 10 J 19.

Treasure Hunt

Write the missing numbers from 1 to 20 and help the pirate find treasure by following the route.

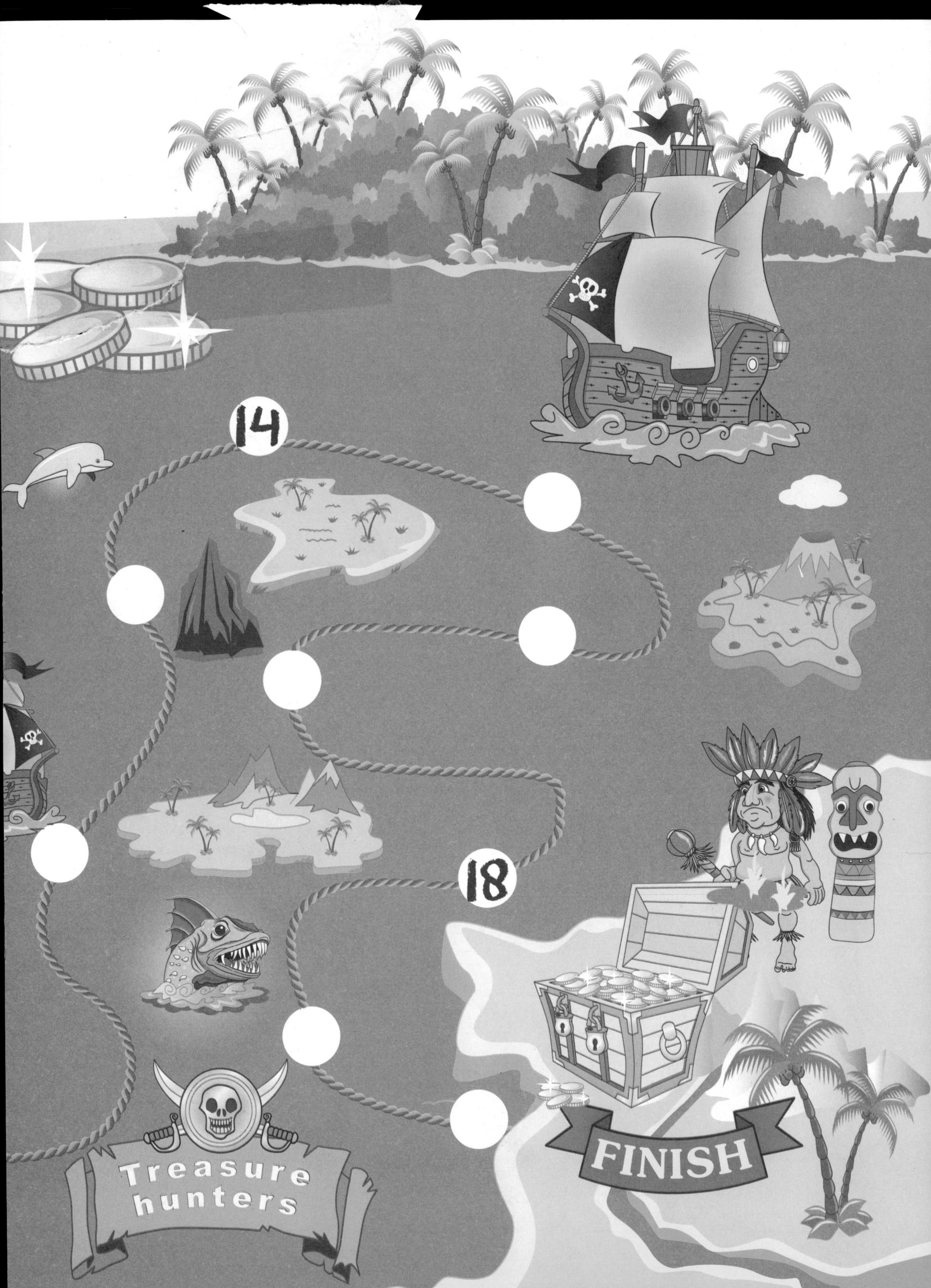

14
18
FINISH
Treasure hunters

On the Tree

Count the birds you see on the tree. Write the correct number of birds in the boxes given below with their pictures.

A

B

C

D

E

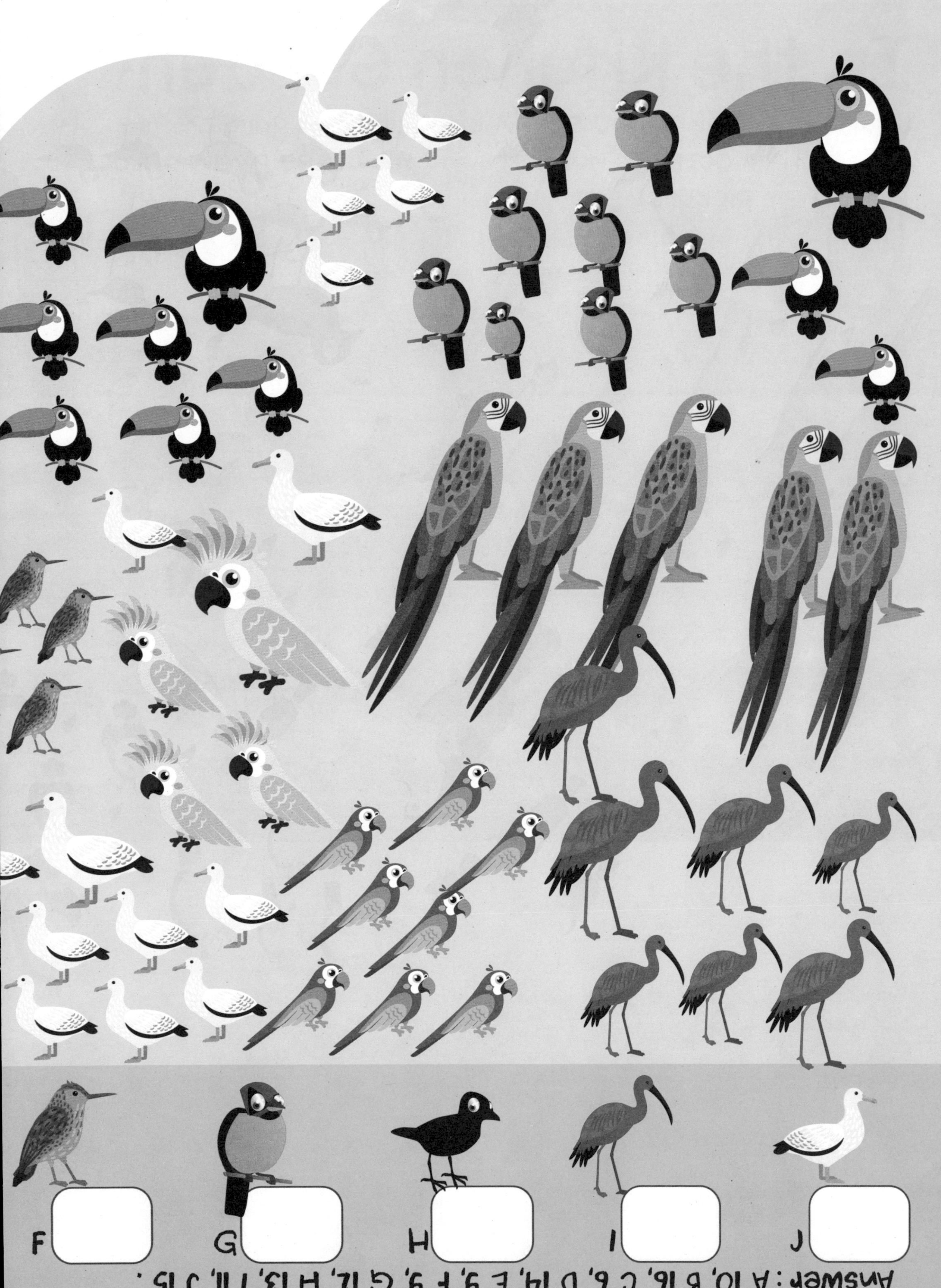
F
G
H
I
J
Answer : A 10, B 16, C 6, D 14, E 9, F 9, G 12, H 13, I 11, J 15.

In the Kitchen Garden

Count the things you see in the kitchen garden. Write their correct numbers in the boxes given below with their pictures.

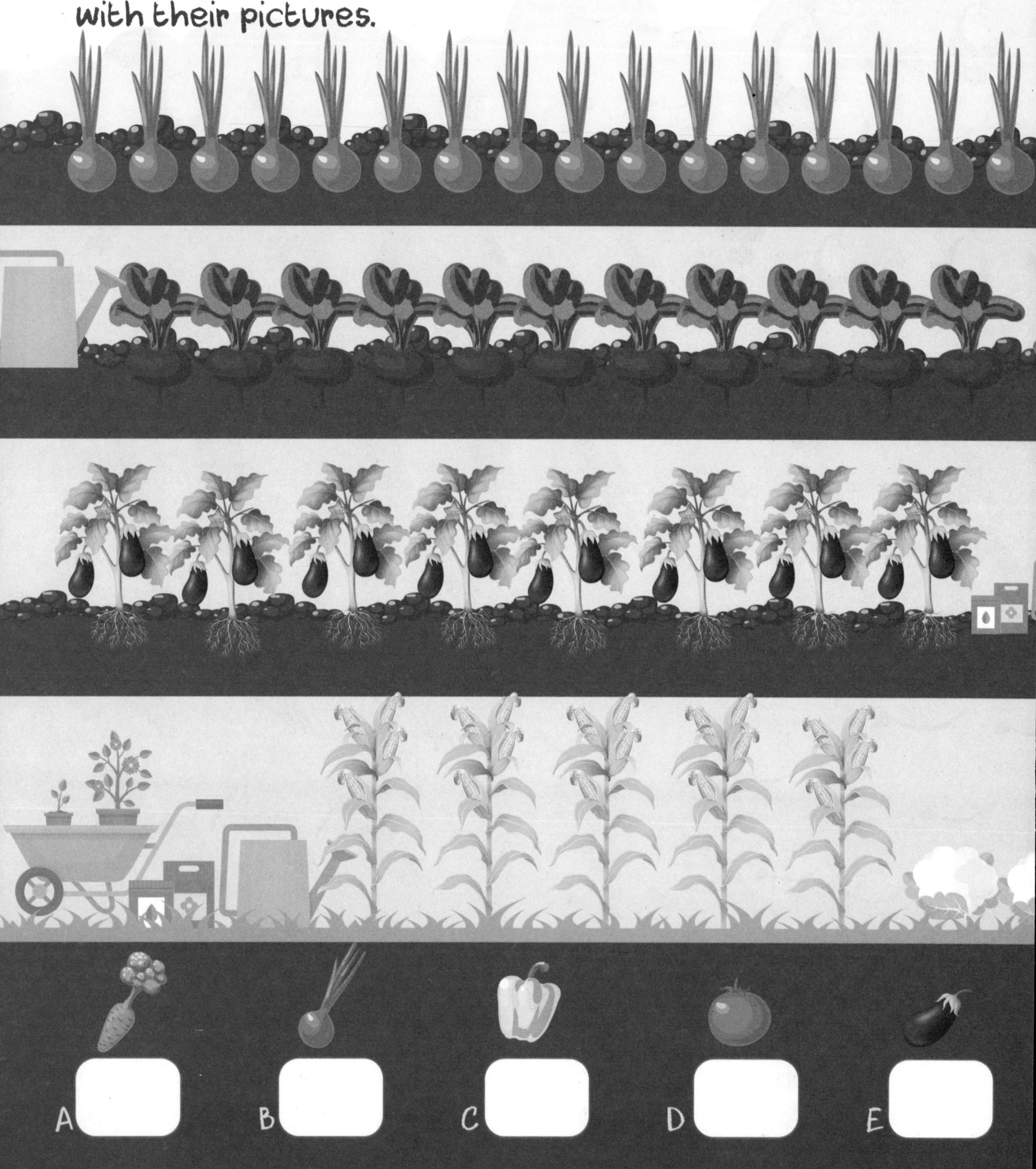

F G H I J

Answer : A 17, B 16, C 12, D 15, E 16, F 11, G 12, H 20, I 8, J 7.

Write the Missing Numbers.

Fill in the blanks to complete the number order.

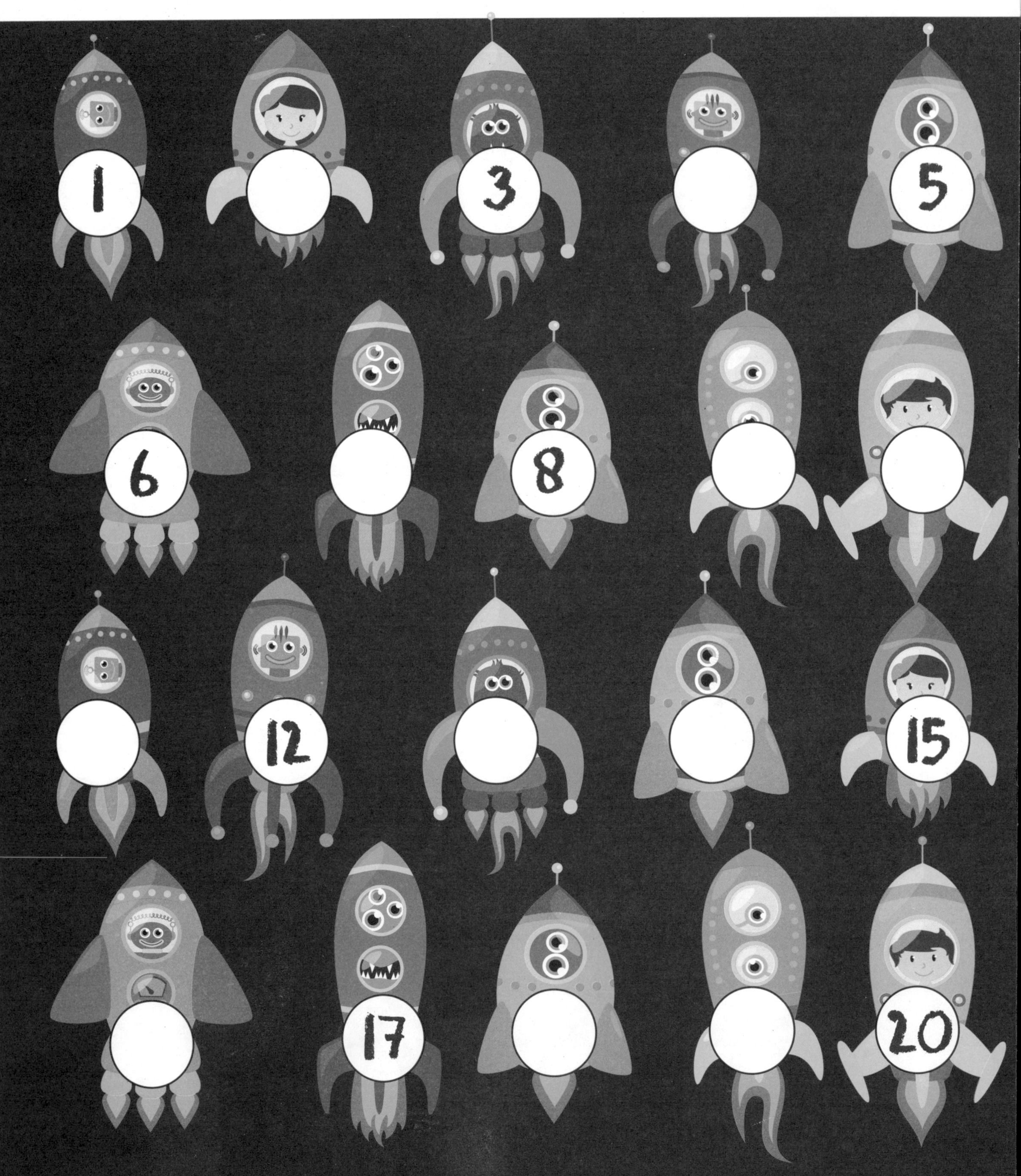